LLISWERRY
Growing Up in 1950s South Wales

David Hughes

First published Great Britain 2012
by Summertime Publishing

ISBN 978-1-909193-07-9

Editing and proofreading by TheGlobalWriter.com
Cover & page design by Lemonberry.com

DISCLAIMER
Actual names and details are given to the best of the author's memory. No offence is intended should it occur and the author apologises for any error that there may be.

About the Author

David Hughes was born in Gwent (then known as Monmouthshire) and grew up in the austerity of post-war South Wales. He is a chartered engineer and spent much of his working life in the hydrocarbon industry, in a career that took him across the world for three decades. Hughes' expatriate life ended in 2009, when he returned to Britain due to poor health. He has two daughters.

Author's Note

Lliswerry, spelt with two Ls, is a ward of Newport, in the preserved county of Gwent in South Wales. It is bounded by the River Usk to the west and the Great Western main railway line to the north. Lliswerry is a corruption of Llyswyry, which translates as 'Maiden's Court'.

Contents

Prologue

I was born into a working-class Welsh family. I want my descendants to know what my childhood was like; it was very different from that of today's youngster. This account took me many years and many revisions for I procastinate, quickly lose momentum and am never satisfied.

It is a true story, although literary licence has been taken to give a humorous slant. It may appeal to those who wish to know about growing up in mid-twentieth century Newport. I tell of growing up, of changing myself from a fat and timid child to an athletic young man, and finish with my attending university.

I am not discontented; I am happy with my lot. I had my share of joys, disappointments, challenges and triumphs. I was sometimes a saint; good, loyal and true. I was often a sod; unfaithful, lying and devious.

1. Christmas in Gwent

In December 1951 the market was full of seasonal wonders. Holly, ivy and mistletoe decorated every stall, along with red, blue, green and white paper decorations, balloons and streamers – even the faggot and peas stall had risen to the occasion. Under the grey of the sky there was bright, bursting colour all around. Huddled in warm coats of every hue, people threaded through the tapestry, stirring the smells by their movement; they crowded, shuffled and shoved, crammed too tightly to slip on the wet cobbles beneath their feet.

Clinging to my mother's hand I was dragged along, trotting as best I could, buffeted by handbags, shopping bags, elbows and hands. Just four years old, I was confused by the noise, the buzz of conversation and the shout of the shopkeepers promoting their wares, the honk and rattle of lorries and vans and the neighing and snorting of horses pulling overloaded carts over the icy surface. Occasionally a horse slipped, although I never saw one fall, and people jumped aside with cries of warning and distress. If the door of a tavern opened we were enveloped by warmth, the smell of tobacco and beer and the carols being played on the piano that every pub, inn and tavern had in its bar-room. Inside the hostelry there was light, life and laughter.

Hanging by their legs outside the butcher's stall were rabbits with their eyes and bellies open and pheasants with their throats open and eyes shut; they looked sad.

"Mam, why don't we buy a rabbit?" I enquired.

"There's not much on them."

"Why don't we have one of those?" I said pointing to a pheasant.

"Sssh, come away."

Mam was thinking of the pennies.

I cannot remember seeing turkeys, but piled high were chickens, ducks and geese; none were plucked or drawn. The plucking and drawing were part of Christmas; it was an expected task that everyone did. Christmas fruit was on sale: figs, dates, mandarins, oranges, apples, pineapples and nuts of many kinds. Our family bought all of these except pineapples, which were too expensive. The fruit we put in the pantry. We were not allowed to eat any of it until Christmas Eve.

On Christmas Day we found more fruit stuffed into our Christmas stocking, along with sweets and the mandatory pink sugar mouse. The family each ate a nut or two, maybe a piece of fruit and then no more. It was all thrown out two weeks later; this happened year after year. I never liked nuts. Despite my vigorous protestation I was pressurised to eat at least one.

"There, told you he likes them," was said by grandmothers and aunties. "Look how he's enjoying that, naughty he is."

I coughed, the foul taste lingering in my mouth, bits stuck under my tongue, between my teeth and in my throat, but no drink was allowed, not even water.

"Spoil your dinner, water will," the aunties admonished. "You can have a cup of tea after your dinner."

There was still food rationing at the time, but I revelled in the chocolate ration of my parents and my grandparents, plus my own. I was a spoilt, fat, timid child.

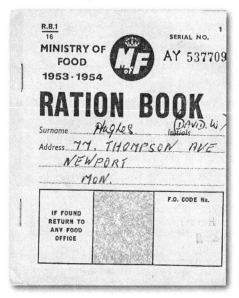

My ration book

From January that year, a few pennies a week had been put by for the Christmas chicken. Chickens tasted glorious in those days. A farmer delivered them, cramped and clucking, in rough wooden crates a few days before Christmas Day. The crates were dumped in the butcher's yard and ignored for the rest of the day – except by the butcher's dog and cat, sniffing, barking and hissing around the confused chickens. The butcher's dog gave them an occasional shower too.

That evening the butcher and his assistant pulled the birds out of the crate, slashed their throats with sharp knives and threw the protesting bodies in a heap. Any chicken that escaped was chased around the yard, or along the street if it cleared the high wall topped with broken glass. Chickens had been known to clear the wall with their throats cut, fear giving use to their wings. The slaughter finished, each bird was weighed. The weight, rounded up to the next half-pound, was written on a piece of cardboard, which was stapled to an often still-fluttering wing. The customer's name and address was stapled to the other wing. Dead and dying chickens were hung by their legs from the rafters of the butcher's shed and outhouse.

After business the next day the chickens were delivered. It was part of the Christmas tradition for children to wait up to watch. On a chilly December evening, a day or two before Christmas, the butcher's small van crawled stop-start through the streets. The local ladies gathered around to inspect, and to gossip.

"Duw, how can she make a meal for six with that little thing? Nothing more than a bantam it is, see. Tight bugger he is!"

"There's only four of them! What they want a big bird like that for? Showing off they are, see! Always the same, her."

Our chicken was carried into the house by the thick string tied around its feet.

"That don't look seven pounds to me!" said Gran, her button nose crinkling on her roly-poly face. She could not possibly have known the bird's weight. Gran was a believer in bluff.

"Well! It's dead innit?" said the butcher, his stock line.

Gran begrudgingly paid the butcher in shillings, sixpences, three-penny pieces, pennies and halfpennies. She lost count halfway through and started all over again. The butcher started fidgeting and finger tapping, with a van full of birds to deliver and time short, he could do without this. Our chicken was now on its back, on a plate in the pantry. Granddad and myself stood looking at it, touching it, me hoping its feet would twitch again. Gran came in.

"That still don't look seven pounds to me," she said, before adding with a smile, "I diddled him out of a shilling just in case."

In those pre-decimal days I struggled with pounds, shillings and pence. Prices were written as L.s.d, which was confusing because we referred to quid, bob and penny. Dad, a constant mine of information, told me that L.s.d. was from the Latin for *libra*, *solidus* and *denarius*. Granddad, an intermittent mine of information, told me that the penny derived from a silver coin of the Middle Ages, the weight of which was 1/240th of a troy pound, a weight known as a pennyweight. There were 240 big copper pennies to our pound. With two shillings in pennies in my trouser pocket, my trousers hung at half mast and I walked in circles.

The day after the chicken was delivered Gran announced she was going to 'draw' it. With childish naivety – and ever helpful – I toddled off to find pencil and paper, for drawing was my job. Returning, I saw Gran with her hand up the chicken's bum. Mam was too squeamish for this job.

"Go away, David, you do not want to see this," came Gran's voice.

I did want to see it and that I did, though I should perhaps have listened to Gran.

"This can go in the bowl, this bit must be washed first, this bit thrown away," she instructed amidst the slurp and slop of it all.

"Make nice gravy this will, Marge," she promised my mother.

Gran buried the waste in the garden, in the hope that it would not smell. Shortly after, I saw the cat of our neighbour, Mrs Phillips, digging there. I hastened towards the creature, which had never had much time for me – and at that moment even less so. With front paws firm on something in the ground, it glared at me and turned from a small, innocuous animal into a huge, evil brute, fangs showing as it hissed.

"Don't go near it, David," Gran said, wasting her breath.

Immediately the thing lunged at me. In less than a second it about-turned, snatched something from the hole it had dug, gave a furtive look over its shoulder and was through the fence.

"Serve you right if it had scratched you," shouted Gran.

She carried a chair into the garden, sat with the chicken on her lap and plucked away. Mam collected the feathers and put them in the bin. With the plucking done Gran carried the chicken upstairs to the bath and rinsed it inside and out. Mam cleaned the bath while Gran returned the chicken to the kitchen, where she patted it dry with clean towels. Then it was put on a clean plate, covered and placed in the pantry. On Christmas morning the chicken was stuffed with sage and onion that we grew ourselves, and pieces of bread that we had saved. Finally, it was trussed, larded and roasted.

It was not always fowl for Christmas. When Dad was a boy the local authorities gave the poor and needy a chit that allowed them a free rabbit. A few days before Christmas, with chit in hand, Gran jostled with other destitute women at St Andrew's school, on Corporation Road, for a freshly trapped rabbit.

Granddad operated a 'Christmas Club'. He made a round on a Friday evening, collecting a few pennies from families at his end of the road and a few scattered acquaintances, religiously entering each amount in his little pocket book with the stub of a black lead. For Granddad it was never a pencil, always a black lead. This money was used to buy spirits for Christmas. He bought in bulk from the local off-licence and worked a deal. People ordered bottles of gin, rum, brandy and cheap whisky. No one drank vodka, liqueurs or wine, except cheap port wine and then only one bottle per household. Wine was not for the likes of us; it was for those who knew things. Of course there was plenty of gossip about the drink too.

"She had a bottle each of brandy, rum and gin and two bottles of whisky! I know he bought more too and there are only three of them, with their Jimmy. And they are not having anyone else for Christmas," the neighbours told each other.

The Hughes family peeped out of the window at the alleged dipsomaniacs.

Where did they get the money? we wondered. *Are they really alcoholics?*

From mid-November we had salvaged and saved: cardboard boxes, brown paper, coloured paper, string, anything and everything we thought could be useful. We made lists of whom to buy a present for and whom to send a Christmas card. There was the buying of the presents after long thought and discussion. Christmas cards bought, the whole family spent evenings signing them (we all had to sign each one), addressing envelopes and wrapping the gifts.

Mam helped Gran prepare the Christmas pudding with ingredients saved over the year. The small pudding, which I thought bitter and ate only under sufferance, was made with ritual and humour, shaped, wrapped in muslin and put in a pillow case. The local laundry then steamed these shrouded puddings overnight for a few pence and the final, cooked product was collected early the next morning. There were tales of tearful housewives whose puddings had disintegrated in the process, seeping away to vanish down the drain; puddings dropped and shattered when collected; puddings taken by others.

"Oh, I felt sorry for her," Gran said between giggles.

Mam forced a smile.

When I was older and we lived in our own house, within a four-year-old's walking stamina of Gran and Granddad's, Christmas was just as special. There was marvellous food and drink and distant relatives turned up. There were exciting shows on television too; you knew it was Christmas if the Western classic, *Stagecoach*, starring John Wayne, was showing. And of course, there were the presents, for which I had a strategy: drop hints from October, make up my mind nearer the big day, then drop my absolute, must-have hint in mid-November. If my parents were still dropping hints after that, then they had not understood or I was out of the price range. I would try again and if no luck, go to my second choice.

Early December, with Dad at work and Mam in town, I crept into their room, stood on the bed, took my present out of the top cupboard, played with it, sealed it up and then carefully put it back. Somehow, I was still surprised when I awoke early on Christmas day and there everything was. One present, which really did surprise me though, was my green Hercules bicycle. I awoke excitedly on a bitterly cold day. As my eyes adjusted to the weak light that found its way through the curtains, slowly, materialising out of the gloom was *a bike*! I was out of bed and had the curtains opened in seconds. Just what I had wanted, but had not dared to ask for. After about five minutes, with the main course thoroughly examined, it was time to go into Mam and Dad's bedroom for dessert.

The expectations built up to a crescendo by five o'clock on Christmas morning and by a quarter past five the anti-climax was at full gallop. There was hope that a relative would call with a flimsy story – "Oh look, Santa left this at my house and asked me to give it to you" – but one belated gift was about all that one could expect to arrive in this manner. There was still the Christmas lunch to look forward to and the Christmas television programmes, but these did not alleviate the depression.

As a child, what annoyed me most at Christmas was to receive clothes. I would eagerly unwrap the parcel only to find a hideous sweater. My mother would take it off me and enthuse over it.

The sweater would then be passed around accompanied by such remarks as:

"What a lovely present; how fortuitous – he really needs a new sweater, just the right size, good quality, nice wool."

I was exhorted to thank the plebeian who had sent it to me.

On my Hercules at the top of the avenue

Second on my Christmas annoyance list was to get a book. If I had wanted a book I would have gone to the library. Christmas is not for giving clothes or books to children.

Aunts and uncles arrived mid-morning, looking uncomfortable and smelling of mothballs. Their arrival heralded the passing around by Mam and Dad of the obligatory small glass of cheap port wine to everyone crowded into the small dining room. We had lunch after the guests had gone – one chicken between us and a tin of Cadbury's Roses chocolates.

Friends and neighbours popped in too.

"Just to wish you happy Christmas, see, not stay long," they chanted.

Really they were after a drink. Mam and Dad were on to it.

"Well, the drink went quick this year. Don't know how we are still on our feet, do we Marge?" came the reply.

"No Bill, you would never think... bottles are not as big as they used to be, eh?"

"Well, rude we are, get you a gin right now," Dad proclaimed.

No choice was offered; gin was cheap. Dad trotted upstairs, and returned gently cradling the gin. He put the bottle carefully in the middle of the table. Shielding the glasses from the eyes of the visitors, Dad made a great show of pouring the gin, bending to better see if equal levels were in each, for people took umbrage if they thought one had more than another. Not that it mattered, for no two of our glasses were the same. The good glasses were kept for 'special' occasions but never used; they somehow just disappeared over the years. Pouring done, Dad stood back and added a quick, unasked for splash of orange juice to make the drink look more generous. The glasses were handed to the visitors, who sat with their fixed smiles.

"Had enough we have, see. Done nothing but drink, have we, Marge?" said Dad, by way of explaining why he had not poured for himself or Mam.

"No, Bill, don't know how we are still on our feet."

Before the first sip was taken Dad capped the bottle and ran it back upstairs, returning to polite smiles and gentle sipping. Each tried not to be first to finish, not wanting to look greedy – or alcoholic. Besides, they felt uncomfortable sitting there holding an empty glass; sometimes they wrapped their hands around the glass to hide the liquid level and pretended to sip.

At Gran's it was a different story. Favoured visitors were given a healthy glass, or more usually a cup, of rum topped up with sugared hot water and Gran's hearty, "Hurry up, time for another."

The favoured few, adults and children, wobbled out to home and sleep. Gran knocked them back with everyone she favoured morning, noon and night. She was often roaring.

"Give him a drink, Poll," Granddad jovially bid each time a guest came by.

"It's all gone," Gran grunted if she did not like the guest.

She sat quietly then, glowering at the unwelcome guest, not talking, answering questions with a "yes" or "no", occasionally tutting. After a face-saving time the unfortunate soul slunk out.

Gran had two ditties she yelled out at Christmas time: 'Christmas comes but once a year and it's everyone's delight, to keep it up' and something about 'Season of good cheer.' Gran also had two sayings that she frequently used: "Marry in haste, repent at leisure" and "Better to be an old man's darling than a young man's slave." These *bons mots* she freely imparted to all young ladies of her acquaintance. Much to Granddad's annoyance Gran also referred to sausages as "widow's memories". In a moment of forgetfulness Granddad might reproach Gran.

"Killjoy you are, a real killjoy, *no harm in it, is there?*" came her reply. Then, in her loudest voice, the singing of 'Christmas comes but once a year and it's everyone's delight to keep it up' and 'Season of good cheer.'

"The neighbours, Poll, think of the neighbours," Granddad might then foolishly say.

Staggering from her chair to the front door Gran would tell him what she thought of the neighbours. Once out of the door she grasped the fence and pulled herself to the gate. Here she looked up and down the street and informed the neighbours what a lot of killjoys they were.

"Come out and sing *you miserable buggers*," she hollered.

To this day the smell of rum reminds me of Christmas.

Christmas was also the time for making pickled onions. It was best if they were pickled for at least five weeks, but we never started preparation work until three weeks before Christmas. Someone knew someone who sold pickling onions, the little ones, the genuine thing, and they were cheap. We went for it. Someone knew someone who sold pickling vinegar and it was cheap. We went for that too.

Obtaining the right herbs was a problem, but there was always someone who knew a local witch doctor who knew what was needed and how to prepare them.

So some old crone was inundated with orders for herbs that could easily have been bought over the counter of any grocer. I doubt that the crone knew what she was doing. I suspect she just threw together whatever herbs she had available; no two bundles smelt or felt the same. The herbs were delivered tied in a piece of muslin cloth, not to be opened, just thrown in as it was. Next came the job of finding the jars. We had a small kitchen, but it took days and much swearing to find all the jars and their screw-on tops.

"Well, would you believe it? The rubber seals have perished!" came a shout from the kitchen.

I believed it, for I saw my family in action. They were capable of sinking the Titanic in a dry dock!

By now we had a pile of onions, four jars with insulation tape as a seal, six bottles of vinegar, but only one bag of herbs. Nothing for it but to open the herb bag, make up four, more or less equal portions and tie them in old bandages. Mam peeled the onions. She sat in the back room, our dining-cum-everything room, a bucket for the bits on one side, a bowl for the peeled onions on the other side and her wartime gas mask on her face.

"To stop me crying," she explained. Dad gave her a look of despair.

"No, it works, I know," Mam said confidently, although her voice was muffled.

Off she went with not one tear, while the rest of us were streaming. Neighbours came in, as they often did.

"I'm peeling onions," Mam told them. "That's why I have a gas mask on."

The neighbours did not seem to notice; they were either very polite or just as weird. With the onions peeled it was time to sterilise the jars. It was generally advised to put the jars in a pan, cover them with water and let simmer for twenty minutes. No, Dad gave the jars a quick swill under the hot tap.

"Quick Marge, while it's hot," he instructed Mam.

"Hold it still, Bill," came her reply and the onions were crammed in.

Lots left over, wonder who wants those? Pour in vinegar, lots left over, wonder who wants it? Put herb bundle on top. Put cap on. Bugger, the tape had come off. Dad applied more tape and tried to put the cap on. It would not go: there was too much tape.

"Take some tape off Bill," Mam said, ever helpful.

"No, it will go on," said Dad, refusing to admit anything was wrong.

It went – the cap was on half a turn, angled thirty degrees to the jar. The next question was how to mix the herbs in with the vinegar. The jar was turned upside down. Vinegar dribbled out. Mam and Dad unloaded everything and started again. Finally, it was done.

A week later Dad tried to spear his first onion, a slippery little customer. When he thought no one was watching he used his fingers. He put the onion in his mouth and bit down. The soft outer layer stayed in his mouth. The hard inner part flew out. We had to sort out the best ones for the guests. This meant tipping them all into a bowl and squeezing each one. The rejects were put back into jars, returned to the pantry and forgotten, until they were discovered months later and were excellent.

"We must make them earlier next year," Mam always vowed.

We never did. Why spoil a Christmas tradition?

Every year, Granddad and Gran took me to the Christmas pantomime in the Lyceum. Granddad bought tickets as soon as they were issued for sale. It was a 'treat' that I dreaded.

First built as a music hall, the Lyceum became a cinema, but reverted to its original purpose at Christmas. We always sat upstairs. It was a long climb up the winding, stone stairs to sit on a concrete bench. The person in front of me sat on the bench on which I had my feet. The feet of the person behind me were upon my row. The rows were steeply tiered and the stage was so far away and so far down, I felt as if I could easily tumble onto it.

We attended the Saturday evening show. My grandparents participated and I was expected to do the same.

"Look out behind you!" the audience repeated.

"Oh no, he didn't." Giggles from the children, patronising smiles from parents and grandparents.

My grandparents would have been disappointed if I had not participated. I pretended, as exhibitionism was not my style.

It was what my grandparents would have wanted to do at my age, had they had the money.

Anything that cost money was to be avoided. People did not have much. Their few, spare pennies they banked at the best interest rate they were offered. They did not negotiate, nor query, for they did not have enough to negotiate or query with. On their meagre interest they paid tax, all recorded down to the last half penny. No one dreamed of fiddling.

"Can't do that, catch you they will, jail and the key thrown away."

They were scared of *them*, they believed *them* to be omnipotent, all seeing, all knowing. Led by the nose, poor people, they knew little and accepted everything. Their few pennies slowly became a few pounds. They paid out a penny a week for a pension and another penny a week for their funeral. After years of this they thought they were all right. Then came inflation. Their hopes for a better future and a proper funeral went. From my birth my grandparents saved a penny a week for me. My parents took over this payment.

"It will do you well when you grow up; something for you," I was told.

It matured when I was in my thirties. I was summoned to go to the office in Newport town to collect it. That ill-afforded penny a week yielded enough for two pints of beer and a bag of chips.

Another annual tradition was our 'selection boxes': grown-ups gave these when they could not think of anything else to give. The boxes were glitzy and I suspected that they contained lines of chocolate that had not sold well through the year. I worked out the value of the confectionery in one of these boxes: to buy individually over the counter saved a shilling. The grown-ups told me that this was not in keeping with the Christmas spirit.

I once made my own selection box. I bought a three-penny bar of every chocolate bar that was available. I put the chocolate bars in a shoe box, a small one.

"That is no good, it has no game," the grown-ups mocked.

Selection boxes always had games printed on the back. I pointed out that no one played the games anyway. But how could it be a proper selection box if it did not have a game, they argued.

Even at that tender age, I despaired of their pedantic behaviour. The games were usually snakes-and-ladders or ludo – we knew nothing else. We would open our selection boxes and throw away the box. Parents would then salvage the box, there and then, smooth it out and make us play the game, watching over us with forced smiles. That box had been paid for so we had to get our use out of it, was their thinking.

"There, you enjoyed that really, didn't you?" they said after our half-hearted half hour of playing.

That done, we hid our favourite chocolates and tried to barter the rest. Failing this we passed them around the grown-ups to earn brownie points and waited for them to reciprocate with their treats.

At an early age I learned to fool 'big people'. Just figure out what they want and let them see you do it, or tell them you did it. Best if you tell them, sort of casually, before they ask, then out of sight do what you want to do. I later found out that it was the same in industry.

Another annual chocolate fest was Easter, but it was a pale imitation of Christmas. Easter's chocolate eggs were made all the more exciting by the pretty, glitzy wrapping. The eggs looked good, felt good and smelt good. At eight years of age Easter lost its appeal though, for I realised that the number of grown-up relations I had far exceeded the number of eggs I received. It seemed mean; that Mam had told them that I was a fat sod who could do without chocolate did not convince me otherwise.

Good Friday was hot cross bun day. Early Friday

morning Dad cycled to the small bakery on the corner of Keene Street and Cromwell Road. The bakery on Nash Road was closer, but Dad and Mam did not like their bread. They had never eaten a crumb of it, but they did not like it, of that they were certain. With the hot cross buns stowed in his saddle bag Dad pedalled home. We complained that the buns were cold. Mam put them in the oven, lit it, counted five and took the buns out. We were not fooled. Hot or cold those buns were terrible – hard and dry. After a few Easter slaps, a Christian scolding and holy threats to withhold our Easter eggs on Easter Sunday, we played along.

"Yes indeed, these are tasty buns and hot with it. Yum, yum, how lucky we are!" my brothers and I harmonised.

Sarcasm is a family trait.

When I was young, Christmas was a long time coming. Unlike today, there was no overt hint of Christmas until December. We waited ages and ages, and then it arrived, BANG! Suddenly the days were shorter, darker and colder. Decorations appeared in shops and fantastic toys were on display. In those years every school had its nativity play in December; the audience being our dutiful mothers and the lonely, confused soul who was hoping for a cup of tea.

The stars of the show, those children who had more than one line to say, were to the front of the stage. There stood the archangel and the three wise men, each with a diaper on his head and a smug expression on the face. Somewhere behind them sat Mary, the bossy redhead Carol Evans, who no doubt had her finger up her nose. I was lumped in with the extras, the rest of the class, the losers. The teachers thought that we all wanted a few seconds of fame and glory. I would rather have not. None of us extras wanted to go on stage. We were embarrassed and scared – why force us to do it? I had to hold the hand of Pamela Evans, a quiet, chubby girl in my class, and walk onto the stage, two by two along with the other also-rans.

"Oh, look at the tree," Pamela had to say.

This was my cue to say, "It shines and shines."

I had been given this line days before. Could I remember it? Could I heck.

"Oh, look at the tree," said Pamela, emotionless and deadpan, and looking everywhere, except at the tree.

"Shiny shines," blurted the sweating, red-faced wreck grasping her hand.

That was it – my moment of fame and glory shot to hell. No one really noticed, as few knew what I was supposed to say anyway. Besides, I was not the only one. Some children said nothing, or gibbered; some broke down and cried, others ran away. Job done, I sidled away, taking a spaced-out Pamela with me. I squeezed into the milling crowd of extras who were squashed into the small stage area. I wanted to be out of sight. Shaking off Pamela I nonchalantly forced myself through the crush to the back, a fixed grin on my red face. All the other extras had the same idea; fixed grins were pushing and shoving along the perimeter of the stage. Wriggling to the back one was then squeezed to the front, around and around we went. Young tempers were fraying. Concealed fists were going in, sandaled toes were stomped upon, hissing threats made and hair pulled. Head-dresses (diapers) were falling off heads and robes (bath towels) were falling off bodies. Clutching diapers and towels children continued to mill, poke, stamp and curse. Teachers sidled around the outside of the mêlée surreptitiously pulling hair, smacking ears and whispering threats through forced smiles like demented ventriloquists. It must have looked like happy hour in that pre-Christ inn.

The headmistress thought it was part of the show; she was positively beaming. Our mothers, though, sided with the teachers. They glared at us, mouthed threats and wagged fingers. Round and around we went. Nervousness played havoc with young bowels and the smell was horrendous. Crying, poking, stomping and spitting we were led away. The archangel came over to remonstrate with us for detracting from his closing speech. Someone hit him and made him cry.

The headmistress congratulated us, saying that it had been an excellent show. Embarrassed mothers slunk out. We were led to a classroom where there was an old, wind-up gramophone and one record. We had to listen to Harry Belafonte sing *Jerusalem* before we were let out.

Our carol service took place on a different day and the school closed early. Over-excited children played and squealed as they made their way home through the half light and the frost. Arriving home they saw Mummy had put up Christmas decorations. When Daddy arrived home he would set up the Christmas tree and festoon it with lights that would twinkle and flash. Oh joy! Grown-ups had officially declared that it was Christmas time.

In the Hughes household setting up the Christmas tree was the official recognition that it was Christmas time and brought about a day of great excitement. A one-metre high fabrication of wood, plastic and tinsel, the tree was kept in the attic, somewhere. We had a small attic – very little was in there – but that tree was elusive. Dad laboriously removed the contents of the shed to extract his rickety, wooden stepladder. It was prised out of the shed and manoeuvred into the house and upstairs to the landing. Mam held it steady and up went Dad, full of hope, with the promise that he would soon be down.

"You sure it's up here?" came the first of many questions, after a long few minutes of scratching around.

I knew it was time for me to leave, before tempers were lost, words were snarled and I was clipped around the ear. At last Dad found the small tree, its lights and its decorations. These were passed down to Mam, who gently put them out of the way, while Dad cursed his way down the ladder.

The tree was set up on the sideboard in the front room. Once the tree was up it was time to check the lights.

This was again my cue to exit the room – for this is when the real bad tempers started; I had been through it before. The lights never worked first time; it was a case of cheap materials in a cheap system. If one light bulb failed then the whole string did not work. Dad had a trick up his sleeve... he had a new, unused light bulb from last year. The string of lights was plugged in and Dad worked his way along the string, one bulb out, new bulb in, waiting for the moment when all the lights would come on. Fathers up and down the avenue were doing the same. The problem persisted though if two or more light bulbs had failed; this had happened last year and the year before. It took a while for this recollection to surface and for hope to fade.

"Bugger, bugger, bugger. MARGE is the shop still open?" we heard.

"What shop Bill?"

"The electrical shop, the electrical shop."

"Yes, Cooke is staying open late tonight. Why?"

Mr Cooke was no fool. He knew when business would be good and customers desperate. Thanks to his experience of previous Christmases he had purchased dozens of light bulbs at last year's after-Christmas clearance sales. Tonight was the night he would recoup.

All down the avenue fathers ran out of the house, putting on coats as they went. Once their bicycle clips were on they patted down their pockets to confirm that they had money and a sample of the bulb that they wanted to buy.

"I'm going to Cooke's for bulbs," they shouted to their wives as they mounted their bikes.

They poured out of gates onto the road and pedalled in jostling squadrons westward into the dying sun, which was setting behind Twmbarlwm. It was a race to get to the shop first; head down, legs pumping, the old, heavy, rickety bikes rattled along to the accompaniment of tinkling bells and shouted insults.

The sidewalk and roadside outside Mr Cooke's little shop was awash with bicycles. The inside of Mr Cooke's little shop was like an Indian bazaar. Much later the last father was home fiddling with his lights and I surfaced when the lights were on our tree and working.

In a quiet shop Mr Cooke sat amongst empty light bulb boxes counting pennies, sixpences and shillings.

The atmosphere of that special day was always the same. Outside in the early evening it was dark and cold, clouds were gathering, a wind was blowing. Looking through a bedroom window, children could see the flashing Christmas tree lights in each other's homes. Inside people were coming and going, mince pies were coming out of the oven and pots of tea were made and poured. There was to be no school the following day; in fact, there was no school for two whole weeks. Young hearts skipped many a beat. Young voices rose and screeched as we dashed upstairs, downstairs, room to room, in and out, around and around.

I believed in Santa Claus until I was eight. I was sad when I learned the truth. However, with this new knowledge I educated my childhood sweetheart, Patricia Thomas, from five doors down. That was me, always ready to share what I knew.

"There is no Father Christmas," I said to her. "Your parents buy the presents and put them in your room."

"Daddyyyyyy!" she bawled.

I stood thinking, *What's up with her*?

Her dad, Uncle Harry, who had gone to school with my father, was a strapping man with a generally pleasant manner and voice. This time he was angry. I legged it. That was my style then: no beating around the bush, no asking them to take a seat first, no breaking things gently to them... just right between the eyes.

That was not the only time I set Patricia bawling. Once, when playing in her conservatory, with a lightning storm coming from the distance, I gave her the benefit of my superior knowledge.

"Lightning can blow your house down and kill everybody," I declared.

"Daddyyyyyy!"

She was off, running to her father, screaming. I was thrown out. No one appreciated my wisdom. I had several profound thoughts at this age.

What is beyond the stars, beyond space, and where does it end? If it does end, then what is the end and what is beyond that?

I tried to imagine something with no beginning, no end.

And time, when did time begin? What was before that? If nothing, then where was that nothing? How long did it last? When did it start? If time ended what would come after it? How can there be a nothing, for even nothing has to be somewhere?

I asked a few grown-ups about this. They looked at me apprehensively, stuttered a few words and changed the subject. I never did find out.

2. Home, Hearth and Neighbours

For the first three and a half years of my life, until 1951, my parents and I lived with my grandparents. There were five of us in a two bedroom council house, two kicks of a football from the Newport County football ground. Hampden Road, gently curving into Marshfield Street, was lined predominantly with council-owned houses. On both sides of the road were terraced houses, uniform in shape, size and colour, all in a good state and all with small, but well-kept, front gardens. Gran referred to the street as 'widows' row', in light of many of its widowed occupants. It was a working-class area, the widows were on pension and those families that worked did not earn much – yet it was clean, quiet and law abiding.

On one side of us, in the end house, was Mrs Phillips, owner of that insular cat. On the other side we had short, quiet and elderly Mrs James. Mr James had passed away before my time. In the other end house of our block lived Mrs Schoefield. I never felt safe with her around. Years before I was born she had taken a drink from a bottle of bleach. This mistake had destroyed most of her speech and a lot of her hearing (although I never understood how drinking anything could affect one's hearing). I think it also made her a little bit "mental", as we said then. Mrs Schoefield popped into Gran's house occasionally, waved her arms and babbled incoherently. To aid communication Gran put her mouth against Mrs Schoefield's ear and shouted. I did not think that this was necessary, for Mrs Schoefield winced when Gran did it.

Before moving into the council house my grandparents had lived in rooms. That is to say that they lived in one room of someone else's small, rented house, which had at least six other inhabitants. Dad said that they moved house often, from a small, dark room in a crowded house to another small, dark room in another crowded house. My grandparents could not afford to rent, let alone buy, their own home, as Granddad was only a labourer at Lysaght's Steelworks, which was a kilometre away from their house and sat quietly on the bank of the Usk.

Visitors stepped through Gran's front door, took a step to their right and were in our dark dining-cum-everything room, grandly referred to as the parlour, although faded wallpaper belied the sentiment.

The parlour lost room to the no-go zone around the range, as well as the dining table and chairs, settee and two easy chairs, none of them matched and all from salvage raids. A large radio sat on a chest of drawers in one corner. A tawdry red-hued carpet did its best to hide the concrete floor, while frayed, mismatched curtains served no purpose. Light was provided by a bare bulb that hung down from the ceiling.

Gathering dust and taking up space in the parlour was also the organ Granddad had brought with him from the English Midlands, where he had originally lived. Dad said it was a Guelph and that Granddad had once played well. Whilst the label may have once said Guelph, I think it was made by the Bell Piano and Organ

Company in Guelph, Canada. The organ almost reached the ceiling and had pedals, keys, stops, drawers, mirrors and ornate carving. I never saw Granddad play it. In moments of boredom I banged about on it, until shouted at or smacked.

At the other end of the parlour, a door opened into a storage space under the stairs; for reasons not known to us, we called this the 'glory hole'.

The kitchen was an equally small room with white-washed walls and a bare concrete floor. Alongside the sink was a small pantry. Against one kitchen wall was a wooden table that took up far too much space but served a useful purpose – laying out plates, rolling pastry and dumping washing ready to be fed into the mangle. Taking up more space, next to the table, was the mangle, of impressive height and wooden rollers, driven by a big hand wheel. The wheel drive was connected to the roller drive via open gear cogs. When my father was a child he had the top of his index finger crushed in the cogs. Gran had walked with him crying and screaming to the doctor, who cut off the top of his finger, stitched what was left and sent him crying and screaming back home.

The back door of the kitchen opened into the garden. Along the length of it was a clothes line, upon which bed sheets and underpants flapped imperiously over the vegetable patch.

We had our weekly bath in the bathroom upstairs and all five of us shared the one toilet. There was no deodoriser in those days and Izal toilet paper was a fixture in all bathrooms at the time; a shiny, white paper. It did not absorb, it did not effectively clean, but it did spread things evenly over the buttocks.

Daily we all washed in the kitchen sink. When hot water was needed it was heated in pots and pans on a gas cooker in the kitchen, or on the range in the parlour. The smell of carbolic permeated the whole house.

Upstairs were two bedrooms, both with a fireplace. On very cold nights the windows were shut tight and the coal fire was augmented with a paraffin heater. We would wake up with headaches the next day.

"Something we ate," Gran always proclaimed.

With hindsight I am pleased that we woke up at all.

When it was really cold Gran put the one and only hot water bottle in my cot. It was a stone bottle and wrapped in a towel so as not to burn me. It was pushed right down to the bottom of my cot, my toes were toasty warm and sleep came quickly. It often dribbled and I was blamed for wetting the cot. I never did but it was no use denying it.

Granddad Hughes at the age of 21, South Wales Borders 1914 to 1918

Monday was washing day: Gran and Mam stripped the beds, piled dirty clothes on the kitchen floor, put pans of water on the range and the cooker and dragged out the big, galvanised tub. Gran grated soap with the bread knife and Mam did her best to dissolve it. It was an all-day affair; by late afternoon our clothes line looked like a galleon in full sail.

Tuesday evening was ironing evening. It was something to watch, something out of the mundane of just sitting. Four flat irons were placed on the range. While the irons were heating an ironing board and a plank of wood were pulled out of the glory hole. Gran had the ironing board. A towel was wrapped around the plank, which was then placed on the table – as the junior partner, Mam had to use this. The damp clothes were dumped on a chair and off went Gran and Mam. Sometimes they chatted, sometimes they listened to the radio. A piece of cloth was placed over the iron handle and a shirt ironed. The iron was put back on the range and another iron taken when it was warm enough. Once into a rhythm Gran and Mam worked their way through the clothes; a week's ironing took the both of them two hours, more if I wanted attention. The big, old, brown and battered kettle bubbled and hissed on the far side of the range – this was for their sacrosanct 'after ironing tea'.

Other weekdays Gran and Mam sewed, darned, repaired and did dozens of household chores. Every evening Granddad and Dad lounged in chairs and read, or talked, or dozed.

Clothing in our household made for interesting moments when combined with my family's delusions of grandeur. Hand-me-downs came from outside and whoever passed on the kilt had either illusions or delusions. Where the kilt came from I do not know. One sunny afternoon Mam and Gran kitted me out in it; Mam was going to walk me somewhere to show it off. This was South Wales; it is not kilt country. I was dragged screaming out of the house. I clung desperately onto every anchor point I was able to grasp, keeping up a non-stop wail of protest. Hands prised off one pailing, I grasped another. I won. After ten minutes – and just ten metres – I was marched back for a slap, scolding, change of clothes and after a *cwtch* (hug or cuddle). I was a toddler, but I had feelings. At that tender age I was excruciatingly embarrassed to be seen in a skirt.

I was taken to Clarks for shoes. They had X-ray machines. I put my feet in the bottom and looked through a viewer at the top. The salesman looked through a viewer at one side, Mam the viewer on the other side. I had to move my feet in the shoe and wriggle my toes. I played with it, bombarding myself with rads, while Mam stated her case to the salesman.

When I was a toddler, a treat for me was to feed the horses. On a sunny day, after breakfast things had been washed, beds made and cleaning done, Mam might say, "Let's go and feed the horses."

She put pieces of old bread in a bag and off we went. After a hundred or so metres we reached the level crossing and cattle tunnel. To our right was moorland that ran all the way to Llanwern village and beyond. If the crossing gate was open and it appeared quiet, we walked up the ramp, past the high, manned pebble-dashed signal box and over the rails of the main South Wales to London line.

If the crossing gate was closed we picked our way through the cattle tunnel, Mam bending and me stooping in imitation. Coming out of the tunnel we walked a few metres and cleared the wall that supported the road over the crossing. On our right we saw over the fields to the tree-topped ridge near the Llanwern golf club. Near the crossing were two grassed-over tumps, spoil from when the railway was built. Sometimes we scrambled up the highest of the two tumps for a family picnic. Sitting there, looking south, on the right day we saw shimmering over the Severn. To the east we saw the moorland stretching to Llanwern. To the west was Newport itself, the transporter bridge very obvious, the only landmark in Newport. The town never had much going for it.

We walked on another few hundred metres into countryside, past a few houses and the Lliswerry Hotel. Turning right we walked down Watery Lane, which naturally had a stream running along it. It was always wet and had to be navigated with caution for shoes were expensive. On the left was a five-bar gate to the field that was home to the horse. A carthorse of average size, he was white, perhaps dappled grey. A friendly beast, he trotted over to the gate whenever he saw people. I picked grass from the lane and held it under his nose. The horse was not interested; it had plenty of grass on its own side of the gate. It wanted goodies first and a head scratch second. It took us a hard slog to get there and thirty seconds for the nag to eat our bread, lose interest and go away. Mam said its name was Dobbin; I think she was guessing. But a safe guess: a lot of horses answered to Dobbin.

Years later Watery Lane and the fields were built over.

Once when as a child I walked,
through tree-lined lanes unsullied,
past streams where the water talked
and clouds passed by unhurried.

Colourful butterflies fluttered,
swept up on held-out wings,
many birds the clean sky cluttered,
the sun above all things.

Today a housing estate,
tar, concrete, brick and bustle,
where nature did life dictate,
there are now no trees to rustle.

Butterflies no more flutter,
children have nowhere to play,
with this untidy clutter,
is God's gift taken away?

Seasons pass in rapid flight,
four of them taking a year,
passing with a sweet delight
and swiftness that makes them blur.

Something else I was fascinated by was the steamroller.
I would stare at them for ages. These were magnificent
beasts, so high that the workmen had to climb up onto
them, and the chimney was even higher than that. My
favourite was a green and brass one, with a black, tatty
canopy over the driver's seat and a black chimney with

fins on the top. It worked in the Lliswerry – Corporation Road area and had an extensive repertoire of sounds. It went forward with a huff, a puff, a chuff and a clang. It went backwards with rattles, hisses and snorts. Turning sideways it shuddered excitedly, then snorted and chugged. Its chains jingled and stones shattered under the roller.

"David, come back, they can't see you, come here, come away, come back," Gran, or Mam, or Granddad – or all of them – shouted when I walked up to inspect.

I studiously pretended not to hear them. But I knew I had to be quick: one shout was all they gave, then they were after me. My chubby little legs and waddling gait were no match for them. I ambled a bit quicker then went into a flat out waddle. I thought that if I could touch the steamroller I might have sanctuary. I never made it.

I first learned of the Sandman at the age of three. I was unable to sleep and Gran came into the bedroom. What Gran should have told me was to lie quiet and soon the kind Sandman would come and sprinkle magic dust and I would drift into sleep.

"Stay still, the Sandman is coming to throw sand in your eyes and put you to sleep," was what Gran actually told me.

I screamed for Mam and Dad.

"If I cannot sleep, will the Sandman come?" I gasped.

"Yes, no trouble," said Mam, thinking I knew the full story and that something else was bothering me.

Gran did not let on.

"The Sandman will come with his sand soon," Dad added.

They left the bedroom, perplexed, with my screams in their ears.

I had learned of Jack Frost too, but he did not scare me. If children went outside barefoot on a cold night, they deserved it if Jack Frost bit their toes. But for a man to sneak into an innocent child's bedroom and throw sand into his eyes, now that panicked me.

A rhyme Granddad often recited, in an eerie voice, also caused me some anxiety.

I come before you, to stand behind you,
to tell you something I know nothing about.

Admission is free, so pay at the door,
pull up a chair and sit on the floor.

One fine day in the middle of the night,
two dead boys got up to fight.

One was blind and the other couldn't see,
so they chose a dummy for a referee.

One blind man to see fair play,
two dumb men to shout hurray.

Back to back they faced each other,
drew their swords and shot each other.

A legless donkey walking by,
kicked the blind man in the eye.

Knocked him through a nine inch wall,
into a dry ditch and drowned them all.

A sleeping mute screamed in fright,
with words of joy at this ghastly sight.

A deaf policeman heard the noise,
and came to arrest the two dead boys.

If you don't believe this story's true,
ask the blind man – he saw it too!

Granddad also had a penchant for bouncing me on his knee while bellowing all the verses of *The galloping major*. I dreaded that song then and have not liked it since. Gran's contribution to our impromptu music hall was to launch into *Oh, oh Antonio* and *I've got a lovely bunch of coconuts*. I think that Mam may have joined in the chorus now and again. Gran knew all the old music hall hits. They were still popular even in those days.

Mam would sing a line or two of the popular songs of the day, *Mona Lisa* by Nat King Cole and *Tennessee Waltz* by Patti Page, as she worked away.

I was in the sole care of my grandparents when Mam and Dad went out of an evening. On such occasions I wheedled and whined to be allowed to sleep in my grandparents' bed. Granddad was always agreeable and Gran soon gave in. The deal was that we had to be abed and pretending to be asleep before my parents got back. When they returned they were never happy with this arrangement. I was heaved protesting out of Gran's bed and dumped into my own.

I sympathise with those who never knew a grandparent, for they truly missed out on an important and wonderful part of life.

As I grew older my giant granddad became smaller – when I was in my teens he was but a mere one-point-seven metres tall and of a small build. Granddad had grey hair on his head, up his nose and in his ears; his eyes stared from under bushy eyebrows. He shuffled along in his faded grey suit and cloth cap; a cheap pocket watch was a permanent fixture across his middle. He had two vices: a few beers with his brother Harry and his snuff. His jacket sleeves, shirt sleeves and handkerchief were all snuff stained. I was given a few pinches of snuff at an early age and it put me off for life. Granddad also had a penchant for drinking tea out of the saucer.

"You're supposed to, this is how Chinese drink tea," was his defence when upbraided.

In the 1950s it was not uncommon for people to drink tea out of the saucer. Granddad only did this in his own home, so he was allowed to get away with it.

Sartorial elegance was not Granddad's style. He was happy with his old grey suit and snuff-stained shirt. On Remembrance Sunday though, he put on clean clothes before going to pub. On that day those of his old comrades and cronies who wanted to, could parade through town. Long ago they had been far from home, in a foreign land. They had done what they were told to do and another war was won.

The veterans were delivered to an assembly point near the cenotaph, in cars, buses and vans, accompanied by wives and daughters.

"I don't know why you are doing this, too old you are, not well you're not, fall over you will, kill yourself you will, silly you are, it's your own fault if you die," the women scolded.

A former officer came forward and gave orders. In their best dark suits – then all old men had best dark suits and their shoes shiny – they shuffled, stumbled and groped their way into some sort of line and some sort of order. They were placed last in the parade so that their slow pace would not hinder the younger, fitter marchers.

It was time for them to go, to walk sedately along the short route. The Boy Scout band struck up the march and the old men turned, some in jerky stages, to plod off. Memories of the Great War must have come to mind for heads snapped up and arms swung. In unison, in step, in time, eyes straight ahead, clump, clump, clump, they marched. Did they march because others did? Did they do it out of devilment? I believe they did it out of pride; half measures were not for that generation.

My paternal grandmother, Mary Ann, though commonly known as Polly, never forgot, forgave or allowed a second chance. Upset Gran once and you were marked for life. In 1911, at the age of thirteen, Polly had gathered her few clothes, wrapped them in a shawl, left Pontypool and walked to Newport, where she had found work in The George, a public house. It was there, many years later, that she met my grandfather. She worked all of her hard life and knew the value of every penny. When I was a young teenager I was embarrassed to hear she was thrown off a bus for fighting and cautioned by police in town for brawling in the market.

It was not unknown for women, whether in their early twenties or late fifties, to fight in the street. If wrong had been done, or thought done, a slanging match started, voices became raised, hair pulled, faces raked and then fists swung. We are talking punches here, by big women. Women who spent sixteen hours a day looking after

Grandmother Mary Ann (Polly) Hughes nee Jones

large families, washing everything by hand, cleaning the house top to bottom, shovelling coal into a bucket many times a day, chopping wood, walking miles to a shop and back again with a heavy load, turning the garden over, walking children miles to and from school, carrying babies, peeling, cooking, fetching, carrying, lifting. When they punched, it hurt. In my teens I was wary of them. Bump into them in a crowd and if the mood was on them, they punched or pushed, and not just once. If they had an umbrella they used it, not with a swing but with a vicious poke.

We learnt to apologise.

"Sorry, Missus," we whinged ingratiatingly.

"You want to be careful you do, no need of that," came the scolding, but fortunately no violence.

On we walked, hearing them behind us still complaining. If, much later, we met up with them again, they might give us a long, cold stare.

"Ow, no need for that, Missus!" was heard from some unfortunate youngster in the distance.

"Cheeky young bugger," came the vigilante virago war cry.

"Ow, tell the police I will, ow, ow, ow!" The same youngster too dumb to get out of the way.

With sadness, I see youths today ride bicycles along the pavement with no regard for others. If they had done that when I was young, in seconds some old lady would have pushed them into the gutter. If the youth was daft enough to go to the police they would book him for riding on the pavement. Few disregarded the law in those days. The law was the bobby and the bobby was a strong, authoritative figure with the full support of the government. Worse yet, Mam and Dad supported the bobby.

One afternoon, I was riding home from primary school with two of my best mates: Robert Hutton was in front on his bike, while I was behind on my green Hercules with Steward Brent on my crossbar. The local bobby loomed alongside from our rear, keeping pace on his black bicycle.

"Hello, lads," said he jovially.

"Hello, sir," we said together.

"Comfortable like that, are you?"

"Yes, sir," we said. Heck, only another two, three hundred metres to go.

"You can control your bike, eh?"

"Yes, sir," like a stuck record.

"Good."

A fatherly clap on my shoulder and we went spinning into the ditch, wailing pitifully. As we climbed out we saw the bobby cycling onwards; no stopping, no fuss, no report – just youngsters who had learned a lesson. In those days the bobby was something – he cycled alone into rough areas and the crowd dispersed, shouts became whispers and smiling faces lined his route as he pedalled along. Those days are gone, never to return.

Cars were few in 1950s Newport, so when one drove by we stopped and stared. Roads served rather as cricket and football pitches. When a ball was hit or kicked into a garden, the culprit, or the smallest if the culprit was big, had to knock and ask to fetch it. Often the resident did not know a ball was in their garden and was annoyed at being disturbed. If it happened too often they refused to give us back the ball.

Bicycles though were a major part of a child's life. We rode them to school, to the shops, to grandparents, everywhere. We put a piece of cardboard through the wheel spokes, held in place with one of Mam's pegs. As the wheel turned it made a noise, we pretended we were on motorbikes. On a sunny Saturday morning myself and the gang would pedal far and wide. The thirty-two kilometres from Newport to Tintern and the Wye Valley, along the A48, was not unknown. Not a penny in our pockets, we cycled along, stopping only to explore, steal fruit, drink from streams and throw stones at cats. In the Wye Valley we picked wild flowers for our mothers, then we pedalled home. If we had a puncture we had our puncture repair kits and a pump on us; puncture fixed, we continued on our way.

Mam sometimes took me to visit Uncle Jack Evans in Heol Booker, in Whitchurch (*heol* is Welsh for road). We travelled from Newport by bus, a deep red-coloured vehicle with deep red seats. The seats looked like leather but that would have been too expensive. The bus crossed the Rhymney river at Llanrumney and the river Taf at Llandaff; I often saw men fishing in coracles on the river.

Uncle Jack was Mam's second cousin and a retired postman. I thought him a bit strange; he had a stuffed dog in a glass case (either a favoured pet or an old nemesis). Never mind, he gave me chocolate. Uncle Jack's claim to fame was that he had once had to deliver a package to the house of the risqué comedienne Maudie Edwards. When he arrived there, no one answered the front door. Uncle Jack walked around the back and saw more of Maudie Edwards than any of her fan club had ever seen. To demonstrate her sense of humour Maudie reported Uncle Jack. To reward Uncle Jack's dedication to duty the post office suspended him for two weeks.

A lonely old bachelor, he committed suicide when I was eleven. He lay on the floor of his front room with his head in a plastic bag. He pushed a gas poker into the bag, turned it on and closed his eyes to the world. I hardly knew him; I did not care.

Uncle Jack's father was Uncle Sam. Long before my time, while walking along the canal towpath, near Whitchurch, Uncle Sam espied two characters in matching outfits, running from the direction of the local asylum. Every now and again they pretended to fight each other.

"Two uniformed nutters, acting funny, running along the tow path," Uncle Sam alerted the police.

The police set off and the manhunt netted Jack Peterson, 1933 British heavyweight boxing champion, and his trainer.

3. Family Fiascos

In February 1951 the Korean War was still going on, the Festival of Britain was coming up and we moved into our own house. It was a semi-detached in Thompson Avenue, a mile from my grandparents' house.

We walked along a short garden path to the front door. Inside was the hallway that led to a stupidly small kitchen, passing on the way a small front room, called the front room, and a small back room called the dining room or, sometimes, the sitting room. By the front door a single flight of stairs took us up to two bedrooms, a box room and a bathroom.

The house was basic: no central heating, no double-glazing, no fitted carpets. Heating came from a fireplace in the front room that was never used and a fireplace in the back room that was used.

Outside was a small garden that ran along the front, back and side. Dad tried a few things with the garden: vegetables, flowers, lawn, but nothing spectacular ever developed.

Dad was a fitter-turner at Standard Telephones Company and was determined to buy his own house, even though Granddad was set against it. The little house cost £1,285. Dad was the first in our branch of the Hughes family to buy a house. After he bought ours, my

Uncle Bill and my Uncle Harry (not to be confused with Patricia's father, of the same name), bought houses too.

The day we moved into the house we took our few pieces of furniture in a dark brown van. I sat crowded into the cab with the driver and Mam. We had been in the house only a few minutes when there was a knock on the front door. Mam opened the door to a chubby, brown-haired girl of my own age. We looked at each other, neither speaking.

"Go and play with Patricia," Mam ordered.

This was the day that I had met Patricia Thomas.

When we visited my grandparents we had a choice of two routes. At the post office there was either the slightly shorter black ash path, or we walked along the road to keep my shoes clean. The black ash was blast furnace slag from the Lysaght Steelworks a kilometre away, and management re-ashed the path every now and again for the workers.

It was a direct walk to work for most of them, along the dusty, dirty, crunchy path. A reen ran alongside that had minnows, cocky elbows and tadpoles in season. Willows grew alongside, from which the kingfishers dived. Near my grandparents' house the reen became little more than an open sewer that emptied into the Usk the other side of Lysaght's.

If we chose to walk along the road, we passed an old cottage set well back off the road. A few metres from the cottage was The King, a public house that had started life as The King of Prussia. The name was shortened during one of our bouts of hostility with the Prussians. After The King there were a general store, a butcher's shop and a fruit and grocery shop, then Downing Street. Across Downing Street we passed Selwood's fish and chip shop and the newsagent before crossing Lloyd Street to The Black Horse Inn. I once made it as far as the Black Horse in my pedal car. I was pedalling to Gran's. I saw Dad running after me as I was pulling my car across Lloyd Street. On the other side of the street I jumped into my car and pedalled like crazy. I must have made all of ten metres before I was collared and dragged home screaming.

Past The Black Horse and around the corner was a clothes and bric-a-brac shop and a shop that sold very nice squidgy cakes filled with mock cream. Then was Mr Cooke's electrical shop, the target of the local burglars. Opposite was a small, grassed plot with an air-raid siren, a police telephone box, a public telephone kiosk, a seat and a green iron pissoir. Public conveniences were common; every town and village had gents' toilets conveniently, but not always discreetly, located. Drinking fountains were common too, not in town centres but on the outskirts and in villages, in the country and in parks. Bordering this small, grassed plot were cottages and a small orchard, behind which was Newport County Football ground.

A horse-drawn tram service had reached Lysaght's in 1901 and was electrified in 1903. Tram rails were still to be seen in Corporation Road when I was a teenager. As a child I travelled around Newport on trolleybuses. The overhead pantograph often jumped off the power lines. When this happened the hapless conductor had to unhitch his long, wooden pole and hook the pantograph back onto the power cable... all very interesting for a young boy, but frustrating for the passengers and the traffic held up behind.

One evening Granddad exchanged whispers with my parents, and took me out. This was strange, for it was both dark and past my bed time. Hand in hand we walked to Uncle Dave's house in Dewstow Street. Aunty Cissy let us in and led us upstairs. I was surprised for children were usually not allowed upstairs. In the front bedroom that smelt of polish and herbs, Uncle Dave was lying, propped up in the double bed with a side light on. At the bottom of the bed was a tallboy and Granddad edged around it to sit between the bed and the window. I sat on the other side of the bed.

"Are you David?" whispered Uncle Dave, who then continued his conversation with Granddad, while I sat wondering why I was there.

Years later I realised that this had been Uncle Dave's deathbed. He died of tuberculosis, in 1952 I think it was, when I was about five.

Of Granddad's four brothers, Dave was the first to go. He left his wife, Cissy, and two sons, Harry and Fred. (We were not an imaginative family when it came to naming children). Aunty Cissy was Irish; how she ended up in Newport I do not know. Her father operated a sarsaparilla bar, on the corner of Gaskell Street and Corporation Road.

Uncle Bill was next off the line; he never married and died of colon cancer. Uncle Sam died next. A short, squat man with no neck, a sallow complexion and slurred speech, Uncle Sam never married either.

My granddad, Fred, followed at the age of eighty. He died quietly of natural causes while talking to my father.

The last brother, my Uncle Harry, died of Alzheimer's disease. Aunty Jane, his wife, had died before him and he left his daughter, my Aunty Gwen, and her daughter, my cousin Jean. Uncle Harry and Aunty Jane's other daughter, Beatrice, had died of kidney failure in 1936, aged seventeen.

It must have been a Sunday for Dad was home and Granddad visited; neither could afford to take a Saturday off work. I kept quiet and pretended to be engrossed in my play while listening to what they were saying.

"Why not take a walk to Caerleon next Sunday? See the circus where they fed Christians to the lions?" suggested Granddad.

"No, he's too young to walk that far," said Dad, spoiling things.

"Nah he baint," said Granddad, renewing hope.

Circus, lions, I was up for it, if it was me they were talking about. I had to find out more, but I had to give it time and be subtle.

"What is Christian, Daddy?" I babbled two seconds later. "Daddy, Daddy, what is Christian? Hello, hello, Christian, what is it?"

A clip around the ear.

"You were told not to interrupt big people." This was Dad's most common reason for clipping me.

But lions were too tempting a topic. I threw in a few pleases to sweeten the interruption. After a few more clips around the same ear, Granddad enlightened me.

"Christians are people like we are," he explained simply.

This did not sound good.

"Why throw them to the lions?" I had to find out.

"Because the Romans did not like Christians," they harmonised.

I had questions; Dad had a smacking hand.

The heck with it, not everyone likes everyone else, I decided. Maybe these Christians were a particular group of people, like gypsies, who had upset these Romans, whoever they were. If I kept a low profile maybe the Romans would not throw me to the lions. Besides, Dad and Granddad would be with me and I could deny being a Christian – I had only just found out that I was a Christian. I made a mental note to ask Patricia if she was a Christian and what she knew about it and the Romans.

The next day all I remembered was *circus, lions, people thrown to the lions*. By gosh, this sounded exciting. I was desperate to go. I had to go quickly too, before the supply of that type of Christian ran out, or someone stopped the Romans throwing Christians to the lions.

Such entertainment within walking distance! Why had I not heard of this before? Just to quell doubts I toddled along to see Patricia's father.

"Uncle Harry, is there is a circus where Romans throw Christians to lions?" I asked full of hope.

"Aye, that's Caerleon that is, see," Uncle Harry said.

Confirmed!

The next Sunday Granddad called in and we were off. Out of the house, along our short path, out the gate, turn left, walk to the end of the avenue and follow the pavement around to the left. Another fifty metres turn sharper left then through the cattle tunnel. We walked across the quarry, through the cutting that later became Aberthaw Road, through the pre-fabs, crossed Chepstow

Road, then up Lawrence Hill to Christchurch. We stopped for two minutes' rest before continuing on our way down the other side through fields and trees to Caerleon. Walking through Caerleon I began to have doubts; there were no crowds, no noise, no vendors.

"Here we are, this is it," Dad announced with a flourish.

What a disappointment. Five kilometres there, five kilometres back and I was two thousand years too late.

Slowly our household effects increased – this was purchased and that was given. Dad had a small win on the pools and bought a television in time for the coronation. It was a small twelve-inch screen in a big cabinet full of valves that took ages to warm up and crackled and whined in the process. We were amongst the first in the avenue to own a television. It took pride of place in the front room; people came from miles to see it, whether it was turned on or not. I was a popular boy for a time.

On 2 June 1953 we watched the coronation. The old king had died, though no one seemed bothered by this; not a black arm band in sight. It was an event and we did not have many events in our lives. A room full of uncles, aunties and neighbours, dressed in their best, smelling of perfume, 'oohing' and 'aahing'.

"Well I never!"

"Fancy."

"Look at that!"

"Did you hear that?"

There was only one BBC channel to start with, a mere few hours a day. I knew the children's programmes: Anita Mills with *Muffin the Mule*, Hank with his horse Silver

King up against Mexican Pete, and there was also the serial *Cabin in the Clearing*. The programme scheduling was not perfect. We had interludes to fill gaps: fish in a tank, London to Brighton train journey in four minutes, and a wobbly bridge.

In the evenings grown-ups watched cookery with Johnnie and Fanny Craddock and exciting documentaries: on safari with the Dennisses, catching animals with David Attenborough and underwater with Hans and Lotte. In 1958, grown-ups country wide were gripped by the sci-fi television phenomenon Quatermass and the Pit. This serial terrified those children who were allowed to watch it, and those, like myself, who peeked unnoticed through door jambs. From today's perspective it was terrible: plots were bland, the acting was wooden and the sets were unconvincing. Today's five-year-old would jeer at it all. When ITV came to Wales we had to buy a second aerial and a converter. To change channels the television was first switched off and then the converter fiddled with.

Before television our home entertain was talking, books and the radio. My parents listened to news, music, comedies and plays, none of which interested me, but *Dan Dare* was something special. After our evening meal the leaves of the table were folded down and the table was pushed into a corner. When *Dan Dare* was on the radio I crawled under the table. I felt safe there: I had the table top above, walls on two sides, a chair on another side and my parents in front. No way could the Mekon, Dan Dare's nemesis, get me. On a dark, cold, winter's evening it was really snug and exciting under that table.

During Coronation Week I was off school sick, so I missed

the coronation party at school, although I did get my mug and orange. Nana in the Midlands, my mother's mother, sent me a coronation crown, a five-shilling piece, which I still have. There was a coronation street party for children nation wide. Every street, road and avenue had to form a committee for this. The Welsh like nothing better than forming committees. I know nothing of the Thompson Avenue committee, but I am sure it was a shambles. Committees are a joy to behold: the self-importance, airs and graces, attitude of grandeur.

The boasting too: "I'm on the committee, I am, see!"

Me, Susan Fieldhouse, Roger Baser, Steward Hayward and Carol Hayward at the avenue's coronation party.

On the day of the coronation party trestle tables were set up in the avenue. Chairs came from here, there and everywhere; the tables were loaded with plates, glasses, warm bottles of pop, melting blancmange, jelly, curling fishpaste sandwiches, hard cakes and flies. Self-conscious in party hats we were ordered to enjoy ourselves and eat the unappetising food. Mothers flitted around, each trying to look busier than the next; each keeping an eye on whatever she had loaned to the party; a glass, cup, plate or chair.

"Don't do that with *that* cup."

"Sit properly in *that* chair."

"Mind you don't spill on *that* tablecloth."

Soon it was over and we wanted to enjoy ourselves, but no, first we had to do compulsory games.

"You will have a good time, or else."

Those mothers with nothing on or around the table, spent a few moments in a half-hearted attempt to make reluctant children perform games they did not want to perform, even if anyone knew the rules. Meanwhile the debris was being cleared away... the mother whose plate had been broken pretending it did not matter; the mother of the child who broke it offering to pay for it, hoping the offer would not be accepted. Mothers hurried their furniture back indoors, giving it a quick inspection, hoping to mend it, or paint over the scratch, before their husbands came home. It was a sunny day.

I sometimes accompanied Gran, Mam or an aunty on a shopping trip to town.

"What would you like to eat, David?" I might be asked, as we toddled along holding hands.

"Oh, can we have faggots and peas?"

"Only rough people eat those."

"What fruit would you like, David?"

"Grapes."

"You only have them when you're sick."

"Oh! Mandarin oranges, then."

"You only have them at Christmas."

"I like dates."

"No, now stop being silly, or I won't bring you again. We will have ordinary oranges like we always do."

"I do not like oranges."

"You do."

"They are bitter, make me cough and bring the side of my mouth out in pimples."

"No they don't."

I learned a lot on shopping trips.

"Not taking him again," the announcement was made to family, friends, all and sundry, when we returned home. "He asked for everything and mithered all the time."

Everyone nodded, clucked and agreed what a naughty boy I was, then went on their way and spread the story.

1953 was also the year that chocolate came off ration. This was a big event for a five-year-old. Mam gave me a florin – a two-shilling piece – and told me to go and buy chocolate for myself. That was an unheard of amount – I had never held so much money. It was a sunny day, a wonderful day for chocolate to come off ration. I ran straight to the 'Little Shop', about a hundred and fifty metres away. This was a cottage whose tiny front room had been turned into a shop. The Little Shop was operated by two old sisters who sold basic items. With a florin in my hand and the thought of chocolate in my head, it was like running kilometres through deep mud; I was sure I was never going to get there. I reached the shop hot and gasping.

"Chocolate please," was my garbled plea.

"Which chocolate?" demanded the smaller sister with the hatchet face, from behind the counter, as she looked at me warily.

"Hum..." and then followed a long pause. The florin did not now seem so much.

"That, that, that and that," I pointed, finally making my choices.

A look of surprise, great surprise.

"You have money?" A raised eyebrow.

The other sister drifted in and surreptitiously sidled over to block the door.

With a trembling, triumphant "yes!" I opened my hand, showing a florin stuck on my sweaty palm. I shook it off and looked up.

"Does your mother know you have this?"

A nod. She wanted to telephone and check, but only a few had telephones and we were not amongst them; Uncle Harry was the nearest with a telephone. I left the shop with four bars of chocolate, no change and a feeling of vindication.

The Little Shop also sold Black Cat cigarettes. Four years later, when I was ten, I wanted a packet for my cigarette packet collection. These were much sought after, probably because few people smoked them. I never did get a packet of Black Cat, but I did have a fair collection: empty packets of fives, tens and twenties of most English brands and some foreign brands. I had Turf, Pilot, Airman, Three Castles, Passing Cloud (a pretty packet, pink with a portrait of a cavalier) and Domino. Domino was a weed, sold in an open, soft paper packet that was beige with dark mauve writing and a picture of a domino on the back. Occasionally I cycled to the docks with my parents, to pedal around piers and quays looking for discarded cigarette packets. After a few months I lost interest in saving cigarette packets, stored my collection in the shed and forgot about them. A year later all four hundred and thirty of them were mouldy.

My first brother, Geoffrey Frederick, had come along on 16 August 1951. I was no longer an only child; my status was greatly reduced and my nose put out of joint. Aunty Beat and Uncle Harry gave Patricia a sister, Maureen, about this time. Geoffrey would later follow me into St Julian's grammar school, where I studiously ignored him.

My second brother, Douglas James, came along on 17 March 1956. He much later attended Hartridge Comprehensive School. This school was but a walk away, near the Llanwern golf course.

Brother Philip Grant brought up the rear on 18 December 1960. He caught tuberculosis at an early age and was in a sanatorium for a long time. When he was diagnosed it caused a flap in the avenue and in school. Everyone close to him had to go to the hospital for a check-up. I remember being given X-rays and tests. Amazingly Philip was the only one to have caught it. Where it came from was never known. Just straight out of nowhere into Philip, leaving everyone else untouched. It took him years to recover. He was far behind in his education and had to go to a special needs school, although he later obtained a degree and a master's.

Until I was in my teens, we paid for our electricity by putting a shilling coin in a meter, which was in the pantry. Sometimes the power went off. If it happened in the evening we were plunged into darkness and disoriented confusion, because 'the bob had gone'. After a few seconds of blind disorder Mam and Dad took command.

"Where's the candle?" they both snapped.

"What candle?" Dad usually said this.

"The candle we use when the shilling goes!" Mam replied.

"Look on the cupboard," they both said.

"What cupboard?" they both asked.

"The one in the kitchen."

"Where in the cupboard?"

"I said on the cupboard, on the top, use your eyes!" This was Mam.

"It's dark, there are no lights." This was Dad.

"Feel for it." Sensible comment from Mam

"I got it."

"Light it."

"Where are the matches?" Dad was not performing well here.

I had long since dropped to my knees and crawled to a place of safety. With the candle lit, the next step was to look for a shilling piece. First look in the place where the odd shillings were stored. There was never one there, for a shilling was a shilling. Next look in pockets, purse and handbag, exhorting whoever had the candle not to spill the wax.

We rarely found a shilling. It was often a case of scraping together pennies, three-penny pieces or sixpences (known as tanners for reasons I never bothered to find out). These were pushed into my hand.

"Go and ask Uncle Harry if he has a shilling and don't drop the money," I was ordered.

Uncle Harry nearly always had at least one shilling piece. His utility supply worked the same way.

"This kettle's taking its time to boil," I would hear another time. "Bugger, the bob's gone!"

Then the same game: find the shilling.

Waking up in time, in the morning, was a problem. We had two clocks downstairs, one in each room. They were clocks that my maternal grandfather had won with his pigeons. Grandfather Knight was a 'pigeon bobber', a 'fancier'. He never had a national class pigeon, but he had a few that moved because he won a few mediocre prizes that included clocks. The clocks were ornate affairs: a glass-fronted case containing the works and the pendulum; a semi-circular crown on the top; side panels and underneath was more woodwork, ornate and tapering.

Dad cut off all the superfluous bits. If it did not move, shine, whirr or bong, then it was cut off. In my parents' room was the family alarm clock, a tin affair that kept reasonable time, needed winding up every day, tick-tocked noisily and alarmed shrilly. As we drifted off to sleep, all we could hear was tick tock, whirr, bong bing, tick tock and trains rumbling by, metres from our house.

Once, when he needed to be up especially early, Dad put the alarm clock in Mam's big china mixing bowl and put it on the floor, alongside his bed. The thinking was that this would amplify the noise of the alarm. It did. Come the dawn, off it went ringing and tinkling and dancing around the bowl, chipping off pieces in the process; brrrrnnng, tink, tink, brrrrnnng, brrrrnnng, tink. Mam and Dad woke up instantly, but not before us children.

Having been jolted out of our sleep we gave notice to the world of our discontent in unison and harmony.

"Waaaaaaaaaaaaaaaaa, it's the bogey man!"

"Waaaaaaaaaaaaaaaaa what is it?"

"Waaaaaaaaaaaaaaaaa I'm scared."

"Mummy, Daddy, Mummy, Mummy waaaaaaaaaaaaaaa, waaaaaaaaaaaaaa, waaaaaaaaaaaaaaaaa."

From our parents room came, "Wha, wha, ohh hee, mumpfff, quick, quick, what, who?"

"What is it, where is it?" babbled a confused Dad.

"Stop it Bill! Turn it off," Babbled a confused Mam.

"Can't catch it, Marge."

"Turn it off, turn it off, turn it off. YOU KIDS SHUT UP!" Mam was panicking now.

Dad caught it and dropped it, twice. The clock continued to dance in the bowl where cracks were appearing and ceramic splinters were flying. The brrrrnnng, tink, tink, brrrrnnng, brrrrnnng, tink, became brrrrnnng, ching, chong, brrrrnnng, brrrrnnng, chung, a definite lowering of the tone.

We were still screaming in the room next door.

Dad must have caught the clock for it went quiet in our parents' room, though we were still at it.

Mam flew into our room to calm, comfort and quieten us in the only way she knew.

"SHUT UP, SHUT UP, SHUT UP," she shouted while slapping us.

Dad came in to remonstrate; around his hand and turning red were layers of toilet paper, covering the lacerations received from the chipped and cracked mixing bowl.

Decades later, when visiting my parents, I had lain

abed in the same bedroom. I remembered those early mornings, just before I was woken for school; that special time when I was not awake and not asleep, when I crossed from one state to the other, when I lay asleep and was still aware. I lay there in winter feeling the chill on my nose, knowing there was ice on the inside of my window and that the wet flannel I left in the bath was hard with ice. Dad was always up first; I never heard him get up or get dressed. First he put the kettle on – it was left full of water in case the tap became iced up during the night. Once the kettle had boiled he wrapped a rag around the handle and carried it, steaming, around the house.

His first job was to pour hot water down the plug holes of the bath and basins, in an endeavour to melt any ice that might have formed in the drains. Before going to bed Mam and Dad put the plugs into their plug holes, to keep the house warmer; I do not believe that it helped. Next Dad had to start the fire downstairs in the back room. The first thing I heard of a morning were his attempts to get a fire started. With luck, and a lot of poking and blowing, last night's fire might rekindle, but this did not happen often. The clinkers were shovelled out into a bucket, the ashes raked out, brushed up and thrown away. The hearth was cleaned as far as cold fingers, lack of patience and little time allowed. Lightly crumpled paper was laid in the grate, rolled-up paper and then kindling were placed on this. It was lit, it was fanned, it was blown. Big bits of wood were added, then good coal put on slowly so as not as to kill the fire. Finally, salvaged coal from yesterday's fire was put on. The fire front was covered by a steel panel and the front of the grate removed to draw the fire. Air was sucked through the bottom and soon the fire was away. All was tidied away and lastly the fire topped up with coal. With the fire going, Mam climbed out of bed to cook breakfast for Dad, in a kitchen only a degree or so above freezing. While Mam was cooking, Dad was washing and shaving in cold water.

Newport Market occasionally had something new. Once a fruit stall had the whole front piled high with ugli fruit. They looked the part. Crowds gathered to stare, some asked to touch one. Smirking, the proud proprietor nodded assent. A lady reached out an arm, extended a finger, poked a fruit and sprang back to a collective gasp. People came from all over to look and poke, then drifted away for others to take their place. They tied up the proprietor for ages and he sold not a single fruit. We were not adventurous with food. Children knew when something tasted horrid.

"It is good for you, healthy that is," was the inducement.

Maybe, but not when cooked to death.

"The Chinese eat rice," we were told.

"Yes, the Chinese eat rice they do, with chopsticks," the grown-ups repeated.

We believed it was all the Chinese ate; they lived off it. We envisaged them gobbling up bowls of milky rice pudding with chopsticks, breakfast, noon and night. Much later, we found out that rice was also prepared as an accompaniment to meats and vegetables.

"No, we don't eat that. Chinese eat that," we were told.

When it came to cuisine beyond the usual meat and two veg, the grown-ups were a mine of misinformation.

"Italians eat garlic they do. It makes their breath smell," said Granddad, contributing his two-penny's worth.

"Why, Granddad?"

"Because it does."

"Why do they eat garlic?"

"To make their breath smell."

Pasta was not for us either.

"Only Italians eat that and posh people in London," said Dad.

Mothers were reluctant to try new things. They were thought pretentious by their neighbours for doing so. They did not know how to cook it either, and if it was inedible that family went hungry. There was no money to experiment with taste and flavour. We did not have peanut butter in the pantry.

"No one in England likes it, only Americans like it," Mam shouted at me.

I sometimes asked to try a certain type of food or perhaps something different to drink. My requests were met with: "Oh what do you want that for?" or "Nobody eats that!" or "You won't like it, then it will be a waste."

Sometimes I was given it, too.

"Teach you a lesson. Eat it now, you cried for it. Else you will get something to cry about."

I had not cried for it. If I liked something however then I *did* ask for it – I screamed for it, I threw a tantrum for it.

"There, I told you! You did not like that, waste of money," I was told after I had eaten or drunk it.

"I did like it, I really did," I said.

"No you didn't."

"Yes I did."

"No you didn't, you are just saying that. Don't talk back."

This comment was accompanied by a wagging finger, or a smack on the head.

"He mithered for that, then he didn't like it," came the announcement to family, friends, all and sundry. "Told him so, but he did not listen."

Everyone nodded, clucked and agreed what a naughty boy I was, then went on their way and spread the story.

I was twenty-two before I ate my first spaghetti, macaroni, capsicum, lychee and fresh pineapple.

Fortunately we had Pancake Day, being Shrove Tuesday, also known as Fat Tuesday or Mardi Gras. It is held the Tuesday before Ash Wednesday. The custom of eating pancakes is suggested by the need to use up the eggs and fat, which were prohibited during the forty days of Lent. I like pancakes with sugar and lemon, or maple syrup, or honey, or jam. I would eat pancakes with anything, anywhere, any time.

Although our house was new, Dad believed it had a ghost. He said he felt "a presence" upstairs and once, when shaving, he saw a glimpse of something in the steamy mirror. My parents only drank the polite minimum at the very infrequent social occasion, neither smoked, and both used medicines far less than the average person; hence we can rule out chemically caused hallucination. The clincher was the dragging sound he and Mam heard one evening. Dashing upstairs they found that my heavy bed, with me in it asleep, had been dragged across the bedroom. After this nothing happened at all; perhaps the ghost had a hernia. It was supposed that the house had been built on an old burial site. Evidence for this had been found across the railway line, where builders preparing foundations for other houses had unearthed Bronze Age remains. The avenue was once marsh; it is believed that ancient people did dump bodies in marshes.

I still have a very clear picture of the area around our house in the 1950s. Looking through the window of the back bedroom, over the main South Wales to London railway line, I saw a disused limestone quarry some fifty metres away. It was once known as Ladyhill Quarry. An underground spring had flooded it many years before and kept it topped up. The railway embankment ran hard against it on the south side, houses were close by on the east and old quarry works on the west. The land was open on the north, as far back as the ridge. The other side of the ridge was the prefab estate bordering Chepstow Road. The hills started gently a few hundred metres farther north. A narrow, deep, uneven cutting ran through the ridge, giving pedestrian-only access between the quarry and Chepstow Road. This cutting was later developed as Aberthaw Road, running into the Alway and Ringland estates.

The quarry was also known as The Links, as a golf course had once been there; then the area was out of town. Which came first – the quarry or the golf link – few knew or cared. The flooded quarry was home to a number of aquatic creatures and was a pleasant place to play of a summer evening, or weekend. Out of the avenue, left around the bend, under the cattle tunnel, a short walk then turn left; five minutes in all from our house. The quarry had a resident swan family, which bred every year, nesting on a small island a few metres offshore on the south-east side. There were a few ducks, as well as moorhens, rats, voles, shrews, minnows, sticklebacks, eels, perch, pike, roach, frogs, toad newts and other creatures. In summer we caught newts, took them home and found them dead the next day. No harm was meant; we were just ignorant.

From September I had no problem finding conkers. The best place was out Goldcliff way, the choice spot being Whitson Court, probably named from the white stone found in the area. The court was built in 1795, and we were excited by the legend of buried treasure in the grounds and a supposed smuggler's tunnel running to Goldcliff. Goldcliff was a popular landing site for eighteenth century smugglers, as it was located on isolated salt marshes, criss-crossed by drainage reens and close to the major markets of Cardiff and Newport. In 1784 two raids by revenue men netted four and a half tonnes of tobacco and 780 litres of brandy.

We did well with blackberries in autumn too. My parents and I had bicycles and Geoffrey, a toddler at the time, sat in a bicycle seat behind Dad. We cycled down Nash Road, then onwards we pedalled, passing Lliswerry school, Spytty Park, farms, orchards and cottages. Out into the country we went to Pye Corner, there to pick bags full of blackberries.

Mr Penn, our next-door neighbour and a pensioner, was one of the few in the avenue with a car, a black Austin. On occasion he dropped us off at a flourishing blackberry patch, and returned later to collect us.

In season some cottagers sold their fruit at their doors:

plums, damsons, pears and apples. These were made into jams and pies. Blackberry jam and blackberry pie were my favourite. Mam's jam was not bad, but she never had the knack for pastry. I had to press hard with my spoon to penetrate it. I preferred to just eat the fruit filling; unfortunately this was usually tart and I so like a sweet dessert. We had evaporated milk on our pie. It gave flavour and sweetness and softened the pastry. Only one tin was opened, for that was all there was. People did not stock up; they did not make any big weekly or monthly shops – there were no deep freezers, no refrigerators; there was no space and no money. The evaporated milk ran out and we refused to eat more pie without it.

"Put ordinary milk on. It is the same, you will not know the difference!" said Dad, taking a chance.

Give us a break, I thought.

"Eat more pie, it will go off, it won't keep." Dad wheedling.

"No, thank you."

"Okay, there is more evaporated milk in the kitchen. Give me your dishes," said Dad, trying anything.

"Why not just bring the evaporated milk in here?"

"Give me your dishes." A hint of no-nonsense.

Dad returned with the dishes: hard pie crust stained with a few drops of ordinary milk. A waste of pie, milk, credibility and trust!

4. Visits to Arley

Mam was born and raised in Arley, a small village in the English Midlands. It is six miles from Nuneaton and was listed as Arlei in the Domesday Book, when the land was owned by Countess Godiva, the famous bareback rider. There are two Arleys within a few short kilometres of each other; Old Arley and New Arley. To aid confusion, New Arley is referred to as Gun Hill.

Mam and Dad, September 1946

Mam met Dad in Coventry during the Second World War. Her mother, known as Nana Knight to us, lived in Arley with her son, my Uncle Jim. James Idrys Knight was a big strapping man with a swarthy complexion. My maternal grandfather was reputed to have been a strapping fellow. Maybe it is a genetic trait, for I and my brothers are all robustly built and quickly recover from illness and injury. For years I thought Uncle Jim was married to Nana Knight. I was getting on a bit before I realised that Uncle Jim was Nana's son, hence Mam's brother.

Mam has a brother? How strange.

Nana Knight was a short, slim woman with a wrinkled face, very few teeth and black hair that reached down to her knees. She brushed her hair regularly and kept it in braids. Years later, caring for her hair became too much for her, so she had it all cut off.

Munitions worker, Winnie Weeks

No sooner had the First World War started than, with alacrity and glee, Nana Knight, then Winifred Weeks, forsook the drabness and boredom of servitude in South Wales for war work in Coventry.

Long after the war had finished the independent Winnie was still working in the Midlands. We visited Arley either by train to Birmingham (with two more changes) or by coach to Cheltenham (also with two more changes) – the last change being a bus to the village. I preferred the train because it had toilets. The coaches were operated by the Red and White and the Black and White coach companies. The sprawling open Cheltenham coach station I associated with the smell of boiled eggs because this was the filling of the sandwiches we took and ate there while waiting.

It was a change to go to Arley – we went there once or twice a year – and I knew a few of the local children. My best friend there was Valerie Lackenby, who lived next door to Nana. Valerie was almost a year older than me and had tomboy tendencies. It was an exciting holiday. The Arley children were technologically more advanced than us peasants from the provinces. It was there that I learned how to make a throwing arrow using a long, thin, light tree branch, a length of smooth string, and a pocket knife to cut a notch and to split the end for flights, which were made from a discarded cigarette packet. With practice and a tail wind, a well-made arrow flew a long way; far enough to chase after.

Arley children made their own kites too. In Newport we waited until Woolworth had kites and then asked our parents to buy us one. Our parents liked the idea of kites and were happy to buy one, help us put it together and watch us fly it. In Arley the few shops did not sell kites; the big shops were in the towns, much too far away. So children made their own, with bamboo stolen from gardens and allotments, newspaper, flour, water and string. Making them was messy. The bamboo was tied to make a cross, sawn to shape with Nana's bread knife when she was not looking. The newspaper was ripped or folded to shape.

"Nana, can I borrow your scissors?"

"What for?"

"Cut paper for my kite."

"Tear it!"

To make the flour paste it was all right to use a cup – "one from under the sink."

Flour was freely given. Asking for a knife to mix the flour with water and spread it on the newspaper was like asking for a mortgage.

The kites worked, that was all that could be said of them. They were robust, but they were also heavy. It needed a strong wind to launch them. Once the wind dropped below gale force so did my kite, and I had to pray it did not land on anything breakable. The Arley gang flew their kites over crop fields, but banned me from joining.

"We fly kites over fields to keep the birds down while the big boys knock them over," one of the tots later told me. "You can't come because you are clumsy and have a big mouth."

It was years before I realised that game birds are reluctant to take to the air if they think a hawk is hovering overhead. Instead, they cower among the stalks and become prey for a child with a heavy stick.

Nana Knight took no nonsense; she had her housework to do and a timetable. Holiday or not, tired or not, we were dragged out of bed at Nana's convenience. We dressed as ordered and quickly ate breakfast. Then, rain or shine, we were thrown out and commanded not to come back until lunch time. In the lane other children were milling around, picking bits of breakfast from their teeth and discussing where to go and what to do. I joined in the debate, was ignored and tagged along with the mob. We either threaded our way through woods, rambled across fields, fished in streams, fell into streams, or picked fruit, or did all these things.

Of an evening we played games. In the winter, when it became dark early, we played knock-up-ginger; that is we knocked on doors and ran away. The gang did not want to play this with me. I laughed in a Welsh accent so everyone knew it was me, they said. And when interrogated by Mam I blabbed on everyone else.

I do not know about laughing with a Welsh accent, but I do know that I quickly broke under questioning.

On other nights we played kick-the-can. We searched dustbins for a can, which was placed on the road and a circle chalked around it. One child was chosen to be the chaser. Another of the children kicked the can and we scattered. The chaser had to retrieve the can and place it back in the circle, then chase us down and tag us. When caught we had to wait by the can. We were freed if an uncaught comrade managed to sneak in and kick the can.

One of the highlights of Arley was Dee Di ice cream. It had a flavour and texture that I remember was creamy in every way. Dee Di did the rounds twice a day. He would serve it in a cup, glass or jug if one took them along. I went to the van with a pint beer mug and jostled with the others until I was noticed. Usually I was the last served, and bought my sixpenny's worth. Back at the house I hid myself away and savoured it; it was best when slightly melted. It was widely known as a tasty ice cream, so much so that even grown-ups ate it and they let me eat it twice a day. When other ice cream men toured the streets playing their chimes, children rushed out, saw it was not Dee Di and went back inside to wait. Our day hinged on Dee Di.

"Has Dee Di come yet?" we anxiously asked, after having hurried back from the fields or wood.

If not, we waited. If we had missed him our day was ruined.

There was a Dee Di café in Nuneaton. One wet afternoon we went to see a Bob Hope film, a funny Western. We had ice cream in Dee Di's café before *and* after the picture; it was an afternoon long remembered and bragged about.

I found the adults in this English village were intellectually more backward than us peasants from the provinces. I was admonished to "eat your crust", when leaving a piece of bread. I never said no, nor asked why, but I might say I was full. Their response was always, "crust makes your hair curl" and they meant it. Likewise, "carrots are good for your eyes". I would contest this.

"You ever see a rabbit with glasses?" some sage would reply.

Then it was, "ho ho ho!" and nodding heads all around. I did not want bad eyes, but what did I want with curly hair?

They were full of mottos: *a stitch in time, look before you leap...*

In a pique I might forget myself. When a wise one said, "He who hesitates is lost", I foolishly countered, "Look before you leap", pursing my lips and nodding my head sagely, in imitation. Bedlam it was.

"You cheeky little sod! Think you're clever do you? Need a hiding, you do!"

Gun Hill's bookie runner was Pip, a short, middle-aged lady who wore a black beret, light raincoat and bemused countenance. Her cover was that of a newspaper delivery girl. To give credence to this role, she carried a bag filled with an assortment of old, yellowing newspapers. From time to time the local constable swooped; then Pip dropped her bag and legged it to the best of her ability and dignity. Nana Knight often reported the news of Pip's arrest.

"I had a bloody tanner on the bloody winner and bloody Pip got nicked," she said.

The next week an unrepentant Pip called at the house, complete with bag, beret, raincoat and air of wonderment.

"Sorry, Mrs Knight, bugger jumped out by the fish shop. I ran into the lane but another bugger was waiting there. Fancy anything on the two-thirty?"

When greeting his brothers Granddad might ask, "*How bist ye?*" or just, "*How bist?*" It meant, "How are you?" There were strange words in common usage when I was young. I recall Gran asking me to, "Make the door to." She meant, "Close the door." Twenty years later I heard the expression in South Africa: *maak die deur toe* is Afrikaans for 'close the door'.

The people of Arley often referred to each other as thee, thou, youth or young.

"How do, our kid, orl right?" Arley youngsters greeted each other.

"Aye an' thee?"

"Aye, where's thou goin' youth?"

"Goin' t' wood, you comin' with?"

"Nay, got t' go t' shop."

"What yow doin' after?"

I was in the middle of a yokel convention.

I can remember too the distinctive, sharp but homely coal fire smell that was everywhere in Arley; a hint of sulphur, a taste of coke and a mix of ash and wood. If we went out of the village on the east side we climbed a hill. Looking back from the brow, on a still morning, all that was seen of Arley was grey roofs and red chimneys rising above a layer of silver smoke.

The village was the colliery; there was nothing else there, nor was there any other work for miles. Uncle Jim was a face worker. He and Nana Knight lived in a colliery house, at a low rent. They had free coal and they had an outside privy with no privacy. If Valerie was sat in her privy when I was sat in ours, we talked to each other. We guessed who had eaten what for supper and threw messages over the top of the wall; we sat so close we could almost hold hands.

Once a week the tin bath was taken off the kitchen wall and placed in front of the fire in the parlour. The bath was filled with hot water that came from the boiler in the corner of the small kitchen. The boiler was then widely referred to as the 'copper', for such boilers had once been made of copper. The boiler was for the washing of laundry and was a red brick affair in which was fixed a solid metal bowl of healthy proportions. A robust wooden panel covered the top. Burning coals, from the kitchen range, were shovelled into the fire space at the bottom. A flue behind the boiler took away smoke and fumes.

I was the eldest so had a bath first. With the bath in front of the fire and a quarter full, I climbed in and sat down. Mam wet me all over and soaped me with a flannel. If a neighbour came in, as they often did, I sat there in all my glory totally ignored, with the water growing cold.

Up piped Nana.

"He's had enough, he can come out. Geoffrey get undressed. Marge take out half that water and add hot new stuff."

Mam bailed out, then poured in. In a moment of kindness I gave Geoffrey some more warm water before I got out. Geoffrey got in, was wet all over and soaped with a flannel.

Up piped Nana.

"He's had enough, he can come out. Douglas get undressed. Marge take out half that water and add hot new stuff."

Mam bailed out, then poured in. Douglas got in, was wet all over and soaped with a flannel.

Geoffrey started giggling. Geoffrey could not giggle more than ten seconds before it became a guffaw. Geoffrey could not keep things to himself. He motioned me over.

"I piddled in Douglas's bath water," he managed to gasp between guffaws, hiccups and snorting. Then the belly shaking, belly aching guffaws.

Well, I had piddled in his but I did not take on so much.

"What's up with him?" Mam asked

"He said he wet in Douglas's bath water," I answered

"I did not," snapped a worried Geoffrey, no longer laughing.

"You did," said I. "He did Mam, he said that." God, but I was a grass. I would stitch up anyone for no reason.

"I want another bath, I want another bath, Mam, Nana I want another bath, I'm dirty I want another bath, waaaaaaaaaaaaaaaaa," Douglas wailed.

But Mam and Nana were too busy climbing into Geoffrey.

"That was a dirty thing to do. Why did you do that? We brought you up better than that. Dirty you are. Naughty you are."

I walked upstairs to don my pyjamas.

"Why did you tell Mam what I done?" asked a tearful Geoffrey from behind me.

"No reason," said I.

Actually I did it because I enjoyed the ensuing ruckus.

Pyjamas on I was back downstairs where a whimpering Douglas was being comforted with a few slaps.

"Nana," I asked ingratiatingly, in my best smarmy style, "can I make the toast for you and Mam?"

"There's a good boy," said Nana.

I sat near the fire with the toasting fork, browning bread. Geoffrey and Douglas were pressed into service to also make the evenings toast. There was only one toasting fork though and I had it. The others had to use ordinary forks, which were much shorter. As a result Geoffrey and

Douglas burned their fingers and knuckles, dropped the toast and cried and cursed.

"There is no need of that," said I. "If you do not want to make the toast then leave. I shall make it all."

"Good boy you are, David," said Nana. Then to Mam in the kitchen she shouted, "Your David is a good boy, Marge."

Uncle Jim earned good money and Nana had a pension. They had no debts and when we visited them, Nana bought a chicken, a real luxury. Valerie and I walked to a local farm with the order from Nana. From the farm gate onwards we threaded our way through golden brown, clucking chickens. The note delivered, we shuffled out through the chickens. Around the wall, eight-year-old Val continued my instructions on village life.

"If bugger's not looking, grab a bloody chicken," she commanded.

The farmer had been born and raised in that village – the bugger was looking, so were his dogs, cows, sheep, pigs and wife. Birds of the air stopped chirping and began looking, rabbits everywhere popped up their heads and were looking. No chance of a bloody chicken.

A few years ago, I bought my parents Ordnance Survey maps of the places in which they were born and raised. The maps were drawn in the 1920s when they were born. Newport's suburbs and district were covered by six maps. Poor little Arley was but a blot on one. My parents spent ages poring over them and showing them to the neighbours. I believe that this was one of my more successful presents.

5. Health and Laudanum

When I was a toddler, I had caught whooping cough, though only a mild dose as I had been vaccinated for it. In the later stage of the illness, an aid to recovery was thought to be sea air. This was something Mam and Dad had learned from the cinema and novels.

"Nothing for it but he must go to sea," they had agreed.

My 'sea voyage' was a sprint across the Severn Estuary on the side-wheel paddle steamer to Weston-super-Mare. Once underway, in the middle of the Usk, a residual cough caught me. After my first whoop I had the deck to myself.

I had all the other well-known childhood illnesses too: measles, mumps, fevers and poxes of many types. You name it, I had it. Doctors made house calls, but it gave us something to do to if we walked to the surgery. I do not think my grandparents or parents liked the doctor coming to the house. It was considered soft, or taking advantage, unless the patient was very young, very old or very sick. People were also embarrassed about their houses and in awe of doctors. Doctors were educated, owned cars, wore smart clothes and lived in big houses. When the doctor was due to visit, housewives cleaned and scrubbed their houses, best things were laid out, chronically ill children were pulled out of bed, bathed and dressed in their best. Our family doctors were Doctor Murphy, a portly Irish man, and his slimmer partner, Doctor Butler, also Irish. Doctor Murphy was arrested from time to time for being drunk while driving.

No matter the illness, my grandparents and parents were of the shared opinion that it was "just another childhood illness".

"No need to waste the doctor's time," they told each other. "Wait a bit and see."

I was forced to go out and dragged around by my folks, spreading sickness. Everywhere I went children later dropped like flies. When it was obvious that I was unwell – covered in spots, glands the size of a football, unable to eat, continually grizzling – my family decided I should stay inside. By then whatever I had was past the contagious stage.

"Put him in bed, keep him warm," they agreed.

I was tucked under a sheet, a blanket or two and an overlay (also referred to as a quilt or eiderdown). It was like being in a straitjacket. I did not want to stay in bed for forty-eight continuous hours. The doctor was called, sometimes from the nearby telephone kiosk, with each trying to get the other to call. They did not know how to use a telephone and were scared of the thing. Sometimes a message was sent by word of mouth, or note. If by note, all heads were together, a combined family effort.

"You do it," one would say.

"No you do it, you have the best writing."

"What shall we say?"

"Tell him David's sick."

So it went on – no official document received as much attention. The first draft was made. Then page after page was torn out of the cheap pad, crumpled and thrown in the fire, until, finally, they were pleased with it. Meanwhile, I was upstairs dying.

"Okay, give me the good paper."

"Wait until Billy comes home. He will know what to say."

"No, we've done it now."

With the good paper on the table, the writer dried his or her hands and the others stood back and held their breath. When finished, they passed it around.

"Don't get finger marks on it. Are your hands clean?"

Hold it up and inspect it, keep it on the table and come back and look at it, show it to the neighbours. All agreed it was a superior piece of work. Later the neighbours told each other, "Wrote a smashing letter, they did, see."

Next was to find someone to take it to the doctor's surgery.

"I will go," said Mam or Gran.

"Then why go to all the trouble of writing a bloody note?" said Granddad. "If you go, you can *tell* him!"

But so much effort had been put into it, and besides, a sheet of good paper had been used, so they would send it. Someone stood out front and flagged down the first child.

"Hey, you know Doctor Murphy's surgery?"

"Yes." The usual answer, for most of the children did.

"Then take this there now."

"I'm going somewhere."

"Give you a penny."

"All right."

"When you come back, tell us what time doctor is coming."

When the doctor arrived, I heard bowing and scraping downstairs. Clump, puff, clump, puff, up the stairs, clump, puff, pause, puff, puff, puff. It had to be Doctor Murphy. He came into the bedroom, Mam peeping from behind him.

"Hello," consult notes, "David."

"Hello, doctor," I said, always shyly.

"How are you?"

Sick, else neither of us would be here. I did not say it.

I had been sick for five days and in bed for two days. That morning I had been dragged out of a warm bed, taken into a cold bathroom, dunked in tepid water, scrubbed, rubbed dry and deposited back in a cold bed, in a cold room. It was therapeutic; I did, in fact, feel much better.

"I feel much better," I offered.

"No he doesn't," said Mam sharply.

"I want to get up," I chirped.

"No he doesn't," said Mam sharply.

"I want to go out and play," I said in an insistent tone.

"No he doesn't," said Mam sharply.

"I'm hungry," I said half to myself.

Thermometer in mouth, stethoscope on chest, breathe deep, hold it, out again, fingers on glands, thermometer out, look at it, shake it, put it away, open mouth, say "ah".

"He's had (whatever it was). I will give you a prescription. You can let him out tomorrow."

I noticed the emphasis on 'had'; so did Mam. She walked out behind the doctor.

"Stay there and be sick," she warned me on parting.

We of course considered it lucky to be ill during school term; a legal holiday to be dragged out and played for all it was worth. A sick child was given leeway, discipline was relaxed. The child was pampered, got presents, friends were allowed upstairs, relations visited. We lay abed calling for this, that and the other. Of course we always overdid it, gave the game away somehow; then we were declared well, pulled out of bed, bathed, dressed and life returned to normal.

The only time we had grapes in the house was when someone was ill. It was thought pretentious to have grapes around if no one was sick.

"Who do they think they are?" was asked around the street.

We gauged how sick someone was by the number of grapes by their bedside. If a child was very sick, the grown-ups did not eat the grapes. When Ian Dunton was hospitalised with meningitis he must have had hundreds of grapes all to himself.

From the age of four I toddled to the surgery to compare spots and glands and swap diseases with others of my age. Doctors Murphy and Butler were stern but kind; never scaring children, but taking no nonsense. There was never any rushing – always a proper examination, then they referred to past records. If in doubt one called the other in to cross-check. Finally, the verdict:

"The boy has (whatever it was). Keep him inside for two days."

He gave us a prescription and we crossed Chepstow Road to the chemist, to wait with the others. We all caught the same things at the same time. Many of my friends sat with me in the doctor's waiting room and stood with me at the chemist. Medicine was free and made up on the spot. It came in glass bottles, sealed with a cork. Often the medicine separated into two layers, with a hint of sediment on the bottom. The thick bottom layer always seemed to be pinkish, the clearer top layer seemed to be brown. The bottle had to be shaken well before administering the medicine, which tasted vile. I cannot remember seeing medicine in tablet form.

Gran had her own ideas about medicine.

"Give him some laudanum, Billy!" she told my father when I was ill. I do not know if he did, but she gave me something sweet from a dark brown bottle. I came around days later, feeling much better.

Those of us that survived childhood stormed through life, shaking off any illness that came our way, our immune system chanting, "easy, easy, easy!"

My friends and I were lucky: unlike some, we were not spastic and we did not have polio or rickets. Occasionally grown-ups reminisced about the recurrence of cholera and smallpox; then they looked worried. Uncle Fred had had polio and wore a built-up shoe and a leg brace, for without these he was unable to walk.

While at infant's school, I had a suspected eye problem that required periodic examinations. Having an eye test was an ordeal. I had to read letters on the wall chart, but I only knew the phonetic alphabet: *ah, buh, cu, duh, err*, for I was taught to read using a system known as synthetic phonics. This was the traditional method to teach children to read and involved learning letter sounds first and then gradually blending sounds to form words. For instance, to spell 'cat' we all chanted, "ah tuh – cuh ah tuh – cat."

It worked; by the age of five we were starting to read. In my middle age I wondered if I had not been slightly dyslexic as a child. Whether I read out 'hypotenuse', 'hypnotise' or 'hippopotamus' was a matter of random choice, regardless of context. The teachers thought I was either being funny, for which I was given a smack, or I was being lazy, for which I was given a smack.

All the other children in the optician's knew the 'proper' alphabet. I was embarrassed by my ignorance, so I said nothing. The optician had to make the best assessment that he could.

There was no respect for working-class children then, no thought for our feelings. Clinics were places of mass treatment, a production line. We all huddled in the room together, watching and hearing each other being examined and treated. The upside of this was that it was easy, by listening to those patients before me, to memorise the chart.

At the dental clinic, there was only one treatment for us: out with the tooth! A dentist periodically toured the local schools. One after another, we stood in a long line to "open wide".

Then came the long, apprehensive wait until the letter of diagnosis arrived. If it said okay, we relaxed. It rarely did though; it said this date, this time. We set off with a parent for the clinic. We were not allowed to go all the way to town by ourselves, for we were not trusted to find the clinic, or to go in if we did find it.

We sat fearfully in the waiting room.

"Oh, there's no need to be scared," we were told.

Of course there was need to be scared! Children sat there, stomachs fluttering with butterflies, unable to read or talk, the minutes dragging. Each time a name was called bellies churned and bile rose. Then it was my turn. Into the surgery, through one door, as the previous victim was led, tottering, out of another door. I sat in the same sweaty chair, jack forced into my mouth, jaws cranked open, rubber mask held hard over my face, and was told to breathe deep, which I did; anything to get it over. What seemed like seconds later, I was slapped awake and roughly led into the crowded recovery room. Pushed, pulled and shaken to sit, squashed in with other groggy, moaning, disorientated children. A hard roll of cotton wool was pushed into the new gap in my teeth.

"Bite on it," the dentist's assistant said.

After a while, the blood-soaked cotton wool was removed and thrown into an open bin. A new roll took its place in my mouth.

Only once was there pity for me... I was called to have a front tooth removed.

"Oh David, a front tooth, why do you not clean your teeth?"

The whole family participated in the lamenting. If I had cleaned them any more I would have had arms like Hercules. I did not understand it: I had not had a tooth examination since that last tooth had come out. I stated this.

"Oh, they know, they are educated. Doctors they are," Mam said.

We turned up at the clinic, Mam and I. It was a quiet day, my lucky day. There was only a trainee there and

I was the only patient. He was foreign – Canadian, or South African. He was young, keen and conscientious. He looked at my teeth and read my notes, again looked at my teeth and read my notes. He gave me a thorough check, then he spoke to Mam.

"There is nothing wrong with the tooth," he said, "and, judging by the state of his other teeth, I am surprised that he has had so many extractions."

He cleaned my teeth for me, so that we did not think it a wasted trip. I did not know they did that.

"Who gave you the letter?" Mam asked on the walk to the bus stop.

It was my namesake in Mr Jenkins' class, that is who. He was scared of the dentist and had a cunning disposition. He had been dumping his problems onto me. I hoped that all his teeth rotted, all at the same time.

In the fifty years since, I have had only two teeth extracted. There was not a mention of complaining, let alone suing then. People of my parents' generation trusted the integrity of the educated and of their leaders. Indeed, men of letters and those in any position of leadership were regarded almost as demigods. My parents' generation were the last of the great forelock pullers. My generation was the first in centuries to say, "Hey, hold on a bit there, Squire."

When I was seven I went in to Panteg Hospital to have my appendix removed.

"I need to buy you a toilet bag to take with you," my mother said to me.

I imagined defecating and urinating into a bag; I was up for it. I did worry about place, position and aim, but thought I would figure that out at the time. I told everyone at school. Raymond practised in his mother's shopping bag. She hit him, then told our teacher that I had told the whole school to do it. The headmistress, Miss Price, called us all together and explained the situation. We were all very disappointed; a novelty had been taken from us.

The hospital kept me in for two weeks. The first week was to reduce my weight; not that they did, for I ate the same as the other children and had seconds. My mother bought me a cowboy book, a big hardcover. Nana Knight came to visit me – and brought the same book. At that age you do not like such coincidences.

I thanked her, took the book and made pleasing utterances.

"I already have this book, you bought it for me," I then said in an aside to Mam.

"Pretend you like it," she hissed.

Nana also bought me my first peach. It was horrid: bitter, hairy and squishy and with a stupidly big stone. I had to eat it while they looked on smiling, telling each other how much I was enjoying it.

6. School and Other Education

My first day at school was also my first traumatic experience. It was six years after the war, and horses and carts were still seen in the streets, as were beggars, the physically disabled and the mentally ill. On that first day, I was shaken awake at eight o'clock, force fed, washed, scrubbed and groomed. Mam was already washed, scrubbed and groomed, and dressed in her long, dark coat, for she was taking me to school.

"Don't forget the penny, Marge," Gran had said the day before.

Lliswerry infant and primary schools were on the outskirts of town. The primary school was a light grey stone building, with a dark grey slate roof, and a little belfry in the middle, though we never did hear the school bell. To get to school we walked along Lliswerry Road and crossed Nash Road at The Vic, a public house. On our right were the few houses in what had once been a country lane; on our left was an orchard. The first part of the school we came to was a low stone wall, topped by high, vertical planks of wood painted dark green. This was the play yard for primary school girls. At the end of this were the main gates. If we had carried on walking we would have passed the primary school building and the school's southern boundary, which was a wall of hand-worked grey stone, the same as the school building. Behind the school was a play yard for primary boys and a separate play yard for mixed infants.

The large playing field, which lay behind the school, ran west to farmland. The north was bordered by a railway embankment, a spur line that passed the Lysaght Orb Works, to what was once dry docks on the east side of the river Usk. To the east the field was bordered by the houses in Nash Road, with The Vic on the corner. We were allowed to play in the field in the spring and summer.

On a hot summer day, wilting infants were trooped out to pick the wild flowers that grew in the playing field and press them.

"Take them home to Mummy," the teacher told us.

Mummy thanked us and threw them away later.

The Whit Sunday fête was also held on this field. Children paraded around the parish, then on to the Parish Church of Saint Andrew, which was just around the corner, by the Vic, singing hymns as we went. We then poured onto the field for games and refreshments. Few of us wanted to parade through the parish; it embarrassed us.

"We did it when we were children," the grown-ups said, as if this was reason enough.

A little way after the church was the railway bridge for the spur line to the old dry docks and after this the post office. The black ash path started at the post office, which had a large pear tree in the back garden, behind a high stone wall and secure gate. In season the tree was loaded with large, golden pears, far too many for one family. Other than the post office family, no one knew how they tasted; we were unable to scrump them.

The post office family kept geese, a gaggle of nuisances, who chased everyone and everything. The lookout goose periodically poked his head around the corner of the post office as he scanned the road for victims. Victim sighted, his head jerked back behind cover. The lookout was able to plot speed, for at the right moment the whole gang rushed out, honking and hissing, necks straight, wings open. Before cycling to work of a morning, Dad scratched around for three or four stones. These he threw at the geese when they ambushed him. The muggers were expecting bread, but Dad did not negotiate under threat.

That first day I had butterflies in my stomach and fear in my heart as we reached the red brick infant school. Through the main door, along the small hall, my classroom was on the right. Windows on the north side started one and a half metres off the floor and reached right up to the high ceiling. I was given a desk in the middle row, near the back. The room was choked with children; they darkened the room. I was sure they all knew each other and had been going to school for some time. Arm outstretched, my mother proffered the penny.

"For today," she said.

"It is free now, Mrs Hughes," said our teacher, Miss Ray, a tall, red-haired young lady who loomed over me.

What was free I never knew. So my first day started: my mother gone, no introduction, straight into it. I looked round the classroom at the fifty or so children, from four to six years of age. I wet myself, and not for the last time, all because I was too scared to ask to go to the toilet. God, the anguish when I first felt a pee in the offing... the building apprehension when I realised that I could not last until break time. Then the physical need kicked in, further aggravated by anxiety. I ignored the teacher and the class; all my thoughts were on my bladder. It was an introspective contemplation that made a bad situation worse. I did not want anyone to know I wanted to pee. I started to wriggle, which was not a clever thing to do. Oh the discomfort: the agony of a full bladder, the distress of knowing what was coming, followed by the physical relief, and then the feeling of loss, the fear. I sat with wet trousers, on a wet seat above a puddle.

"Miss, please Miss, please! This boy wet himself, Miss. It's all on the floor Miss," voices erupted from all around me.

The pointing fingers, the looks of disgust and later the giggles when Miss told me to go home and change. The long, bow-legged walk home, miserable in my wet pants and loneliness, thinking what to tell Mam. She was usually sympathetic; she had become fed up with asking me why. In clean trousers I walked back to school and into a barrage of laughter, mockery and teasing.

We used slate and chalk for the whole of my time in the infants. I disliked the feel of chalk and the sound of it grating on the slate. I particularly disliked the body odour of some of the children. I had a bath and changed my clothes once a week, whether I needed to or not. I expected others to do the same.

My first year of primary school was 1954. Classes contained close on forty children and we wrote with pencils until our final year, then we used dipping pens.

The ink monitor, one of the more reliable and least clumsy of the children, mixed the ink with the right amount of water and filled the inkwells every Monday. He kept his hands clean, but not much else. If we ran short of ink Miss topped us up, begrudgingly. Left-handedness was not allowed; the 'lefties' were slapped whenever they wrote with their left hand. When they wrote with their right hand they were slapped for being slow and slapped again for having untidy writing.

Some classrooms had coal-fired, pot-bellied stoves, with a black exhaust flue leading up through the ceiling. Teachers warmed our milk around it during winter. The School Milk Act of 1946 had given one-third of a pint of milk free to all pupils under eighteen and it had to be drunk. We drank it through a paper straw that was prone to unravelling. I liked cold milk, I liked hot milk with sugar. I did not like tepid milk, but no vote was taken. I gagged on every mouthful.

The primary school headmaster was Mr Bale, a kindly old man, always with a cheery greeting and a smile. He wore a suit and a bow tie, and on his rare visits to a classroom he gently asked a few questions and rewarded correct answers with a sweet and a pat on the head. Wrong answers he acknowledged with a pat on the head and gentle imparting of the correct answer.

Our first year primary school teacher was Miss Eriksson, a big woman well past middle age, with silver hair plaited back in a bun. Stern-faced, she wore glasses, a cardigan and a skirt down to the floor. She had a long mental list of *dos* and *do nots*, which we were expected to know. The punishment for each infringement was a slap.

A class of forty sat still and quiet, not daring to make a noise or fidget, learning by rote, chanting in unison, concentrating, avoiding eye contact when a question was asked. Voluntary learning took place at home to avoid scorn and pain at school.

Every Monday morning we had to demonstrate our knowledge of the multiplication tables. Two children were picked to stand at the front of the class. One child was told to say, for instance, the seven times table, the other the nine times, then each row was nominated another table. When Miss Eriksson gave the word, we were off. She had a mental metronome with which we had to keep in time; no slowing, no gabbling, no rushing. The Lord help anyone who made a mistake, hesitated or coughed. If I thought I was going to be picked to stand at the front, I asked to go to the toilet. There I lingered to avoid having to demonstrate my lack of knowledge. I succeeded with this strategy for a while, until Miss Eriksson told Patricia's mother, Aunty Beat, who told Mam. After this I had to practise tables at home. After two weeks I knew them and had a confidence that surprised me.

It was in this year that I learnt that grown-ups – Mam, Dad, Gran, Granddad, Aunty Beat, Uncle Harry, all of them – had not always been grown-ups. Once they had been children! At first I did not believe this; I asked a lot of people to confirm this strange and scary fact. It was true, and it took me a while to accept it.

Every year we moved up a class and every year the teacher would check our full names, date of birth and current address. The teacher went through his register:

"Evans, what's your name, birthday and where do you live?" he demanded.

We had been given our names by our doting parents, who had taken the opportunity to saddle us with hidden corkers, whether out of illusions of grandeur or plain spite.

Child by child, around the class we went, whispers and giggles following the stranger middle names. David Hughes is an apt name for someone with a Welsh accent and living in Wales. In order to better integrate I sometimes call myself Dai, depending upon location and circumstances. For instance, on a Saturday night in Cardiff, after Wales has lost a rugby match to England, then David Hughes is a good name to have, Dai Hughes even better – whereas Claude Chomley is something best not mentioned.

"Hughes, your turn. Don't whisper boy, quickly now," shouted the teacher, who was enjoying himself as much as those children with plain, common names.

"David Warwick," I had to say to whoops of joy from all around. The best one yet! A giggling teacher asked me to spell it.

What was my mother thinking when she came up with this? It may be useful if the English ever invade. Putting on my strongest Welsh accent I shall shout, "I am Dai Hughes. Follow me to the barricade boyos."

If we are hard pressed I shall nip over the wall, put on my plummy accent and say: "Hello chaps, my name is David Warwick. I know a safe way in, after you."

I have always been political. Some call me a two-faced, selfish, double-crossing liar, but political is shorter and says it all.

Mid-afternoon, if Miss Eriksson sensed our attention was elsewhere, she had us pack up and told us to rest our heads on our arms; then she told us stories. We sat enthralled. She could make one story last for days.

I remember two stories in particular: one was of Hereward the Wake, which took three or more days to tell, the other was of the Ghost of Eve Roberts, which took equally long. The ghost story was of particular interest to us, for it was set at the Farmer's Arms, an inn midway between our school and Goldcliff, with its few houses and farms near the seawall. The inn was established in the nineteenth century when the area was sparsely populated, nothing more than a few farms. One of the few locals who could have afforded the price of a pint then was a Mr Roberts, who owned the local post office and had a daughter, Eve.

Local legend has it that Eve worked and died in the Farmer's Arms. After poor Eve's death, the slamming of crockery, banging of furniture and clanging of fire-irons each night disturbed the sleep of the occupants.

Miss Eriksson continued the story:

"One night the spectre of a woman in white was glimpsed leaving the local church. It looked like Eve Roberts. Clergy were called from near and far and with bell, book and candle, they turned up to exorcise the ghost. When Eve's name was called, the ghost appeared in the church aisle. The clergy beseeched, cajoled and commanded her to be gone hence, to the land of shades. Eve took the hint and about-faced. The assembled locals, for some reason, took up the hue and cry. Having none of this Eve hitched up her phantom dress and hared off northwards, with the pack in hot pursuit. A few kilometres later, around the village of Maindee, Eve became fed up with it all – perhaps she had things to do – and took a header into a nearby well."

The well became known as Ffynnon Efa, meaning Eve's Well. Since then, this district of Newport has been known as Eveswell.

The Farmer's Arms to Eveswell, in a straight line, is a heck of a way. To run the straight line distance, on a hard road, in daylight, in good conditions, is asking a lot of anyone who is not a trained athlete. To run it in a zigzag, across marsh and over hedgerow, at night, in misty conditions, wearing hobnail boots, is nothing but impressive.

Why did a ghost leg it, instead of merely vanishing? Why did superstitious yokels dare go near a ghost, let alone chase one? How did they think they would catch it? If they caught it, what would they have done with it, since they wanted it gone in the first place? With no television it was a night out for them, I suppose, something different to do, something to talk about. It justified trudging back to the Farmer's Arms afterwards, for a long drinking session.

By the age of nine we knew our tables from the two to the twelve; we were able to spell words like 'gymnasium' and 'accommodation'; we read newspapers; we were able to add, subtract, divide and multiply. We went at the speed of the brightest and everyone else had to keep up. Give special attention to the slower learners? No way. No one was expelled during all my time at school, from age five to fifteen; no one dared to misbehave enough to warrant that. If a teacher hit you, you prayed your parents did not find out, because they would hit you too. Might was right and the iron fist ruled. The only right we had was the right to breathe.

Monday morning at school was saving stamp time. We collected green three-penny or blue six-penny stamps, with the faces of Prince Charles and Princess Anne respectively. Every Monday I bought two of the three-penny stamps, which I later took home and stuck into my stamp book, to save for my summer holiday. Once a year Dad walked me and my book to the post office to cash in my stamps, which amounted to a whole pound.

On Monday mornings we lined up at school, gave our order and paid our money. While we read quietly to ourselves, the teachers gathered around and produced a list of how many of each stamp were to be purchased. The list and money were given to a boy in the eldest class who, with another boy, walked the quiet two hundred metres to the post office to purchase the stamps.

I often went on the stamp run, until I blew it. I was with Christopher Ford, a classmate and friend. On the way back I saw one of the houses had a big doorbell. Temptation always got the better of me, and I pressed the bell. Christopher was already sprinting the fifty metres back to school, clutching the stamps, but I had been seen. The lady telephoned Mr Bale and I was given hell.

Teachers always asked the most difficult question first: "Why did you do it?"

Did they want a child to answer, "Because I am naughty"?

"The devil made me do it. I have trouble resisting temptation. I felt the need to express my freedom of choice in an appropriate artistic manner," I could have said.

But no, we just stood there and blamed each other.

One afternoon, as we were leaving school, Christopher nudged me, slipped a scrappy piece of paper into my hand and whispered that I must read it later, at home. I was intrigued.

"Do you want to join our gang we are the Black Hand Gang," it said.

Of course I wanted to join, but I thought it strange as I was already in this gang, whose other members were Christopher, Steward and Robert. Then the paper was snatched out of my hand.

"You are not joining any gang," my mother started. "Gangs are naughty. You will get into trouble. You can play with Christopher, Steward and Robert. I will tell your father."

When Dad arrived home he got it before the door had closed after him.

"David is going to join a gang. Tell him Bill, tell him how naughty he is and what gangs do," said Mam.

"You are not joining any gang," said Dad. "Gangs are naughty. You will get into trouble. Why do you want to join a gang? You can play with Christopher, Steward and Robert. You go near this gang and I shall hit you."

Granddad arrived later and he was immediately indoctrinated.

"You must not join a gang, David. Gangs are naughty. You will get into trouble. Why do you want to join a gang?" he sang from the same sheet.

Every time I tried to explain I was drowned out by repetitions of their arguments.

Later still, Christopher knocked on the front door, with Steward and Robert lurking behind him. Mam called me from the front door.

"David, go out and play with Christopher, Steward and Robert," she ordered.

"My parents won't let me play with you," I shouted to my friends from the hallway.

There was much consternation and flapping in the house.

"I did not say that!" snapped Mam.

"Nor me," snarled Dad.

"You did," said I. "You said I must stay away from the Black Hand Gang."

"This is Christopher, Steward and Robert," Mam said angrily.

"We are the Black Hand Gang," said Christopher proudly.

"Our headquarters is my father's garden shed," added Robert with an air of importance.

"Sometimes it is our garage," said Steward, seeking some glory.

I kept quiet. Mam had painted herself into a corner. I waited to see what she would do next.

"Go out David," said Mam weakly.

"But you said not to play with them," I said loudly. "You and Dad said not to play with gangs, didn't you Dad? Granddad, didn't Dad say that?" Gosh but I was enjoying this.

"We can change our name to the Black Hand Group," said Christopher helpfully.

"Mam, Dad, is it okay if I join a group?" I shouted.

"Just go out," said Mam quietly.

Next to the parish was the timber meeting hall that straddled a wide reen. The word 'reen' (also rean) comes from the Old English 'ryne'; it is a drainage ditch. Sunday School was held there, and it smelt of what it was: old books, old wood and musty curtains. The Sunday School Christmas party was held there too. To earn our party we had to play games. I once won a small box of chocolates playing musical chairs. I cheated.

On a hot summer's Sunday afternoon the droning of the sermon had a somnolent effect upon the young congregation. Eyes closing, head nodding, I looked down pretending to pray. Between snatches of sleep and gaps between the floorboards I gazed at the reen. Through the clear, shallow water I saw minnows, sticklebacks and elvers (which we called cocky elbows) hiding from the brightly coloured kingfishers with dazzling blue jacket and orange vest, such beautiful birds.

I went to school five days a week, so why go to another school on a Sunday, was my feeling. I learned nothing. Perhaps my parents sent me for the sake of my soul, or believed they did. Perhaps they sent me because they too had gone to Sunday School. I think they sent me because our 'betters' exerted social dominance. My parents were susceptible to peer pressure.

For me it was a wasted weekend. The glorious, joyous, light-hearted feeling of a Friday after school and the pleasure of a Saturday morning were marred by the thought of Sunday. Sunday was a nothing day: out of bed late, do not go anywhere, for I must be in Sunday School at three o'clock. Eat Sunday lunch – *the* meal of the week – but without enjoying it because I must go to Sunday School afterwards.

All my friends were long gone on their bikes, cycling through country lanes, sweating in the warmth, seeing new things and unsuccessfully trying to catch rabbits and trout. And I a slave of someone else's conscience. I washed, dressed and went to church. Every week it was the same old routine: come going home time, some old fool was still preaching. Finally it was finished, I was out and galloped home, where I quickly changed out of my Sunday clothes.

"Go out and play," I was told.

It was pointless, my friends might be anywhere.

"Go on, get on your bike and go and join them then."

Where? North, south, east or west? Just around the corner or miles away? Lonely and listless I waited in the avenue.

"He wanted to go and play, now he doesn't. Children, hey," Mam tutted.

Around five o'clock my friends came back, sweat stained, chattering, laughing, carrying trophies, telling tales of what they had done that day. I went to join them, but I was not welcome. What joys and pleasures could I share in? What experience of the day could I recount? They went in for their tea, arranging to meet in the avenue at six o'clock. I was not invited. I stayed in the house, hearing them laughing and playing outside.

"You must have upset them," said Mam. "They will not play with you."

As soon as I could, I ditched Sunday School.

In my second year of primary school, Mam asked me, "Would you like to join the Cubs that Roger Baser is in?"

Roger, a shy, quiet boy, was my neighbour from six houses away.

I didn't really, but it was a rhetorical question. Another evening of my week squandered in pampering to the whims of others. I never liked organisation, organisations or working to a timetable. I preferred to be left to myself, to do what I wanted, when I wanted, how I wanted. Nevertheless, I was conscripted into the Newport 33rd Cub pack and I had a uniform in which to pose before simpering female relations. In those days there was something about males in uniform and paramilitary organisations.

On Tuesday evenings Roger and I, resplendently clad, caught the bus to Clarence Place and walked past the Odeon cinema and under the railway bridge to our Scout and Cub hut.

Cubs had its good points and collecting jumble was one. We walked the street, posting leaflets through the doors of prosperous-looking houses, asking them to prepare any unwanted junk for us to collect the following week. The next week we pulled our hand cart along the same streets, calling door to door to collect the loot. One never knew what might be forthcoming; it was exciting, like a lottery. Junk, big items and breakables went on the hand cart. If no one was watching, the interesting and small things went in pockets or under jumpers.

Walking home on a winter's evening we shone our torches into space and flashed rude Morse code messages for aliens to read. We thought the aliens would never catch us and if they did, we would blame someone else. There were stars galore, hundreds of them, thousands of them – too many to guess at or count. We sometimes sat on a wall, in the cold, just to stare at the stars.

Skipper Jennings was head of the Boy Scouts and, I presume, the Cubs also, for Akela, our leader, deferred to him. Skipper was a middle-aged, short, wiry man; a disciplinarian. I remember thinking that his Scout uniform did not suit him, for he had spindly legs. I had not been a Cub for long when Skipper announced that there would be a day camp the coming Saturday, for Scouts and Cubs. Those interested were to report to the Scout hut at an ungodly hour with sandwiches, two teaspoons of tea, two teaspoons of sugar and sixpence for bus fare. It sounded strange to me, but I was not bothered for I had decided not to go. Saturdays were for me and early morning was for staying in bed.

Roger told his mother though, who told my mother, and then I'd had it. Mam told me I was going.

"Do you good, it will, David," she said, a favourite line of hers. "Besides, I don't want you around the house all the time."

Dad weighed in and gave me sixpence for the bus fare. I tried for a shilling, but Roger had already told his mother the whole story. I had a clip for lying and another clip for wanting to cheat my father out of sixpence. I had a lot of clips in those days; I won some, I lost some.

Saturday morning I was turned out of bed early, marched to the bathroom and made to swill. Still damp, I was given two minutes to don my Cub regalia and report downstairs for breakfast. Breakfast over, a paper bag, containing sandwiches, tea and sugar, was thrust into my hand before I was pushed out of the front door.

Roger was ejected from his house and off we went.

"Have you got the sixpence? Don't lose it," was Mam's farewell.

We walked the few kilometres to the Scout hut and hung around with others until Skipper turned up and collected our sixpences. It was only a three-minute walk to the bus stop, where we impatiently awaited the bus, paper bags falling apart in our sweaty hands. When the bus finally came, we barged on and charged upstairs to sit at the front and gape. Skipper paid the bus fare as we drove out of town on the road to Chepstow. On we drove, and on and on, chattering away amongst ourselves and being clipped by Skipper when we inadvertently uttered a rude word. In the countryside, up sprang Skipper. He grabbed the billy can and started downstairs.

"Follow me boys and don't fall down," he called.

We trooped off the bus in disorder to follow Skipper and the billy can through a gate, then over a stile, along a narrow, nettle-lined track, then across a field. We walked along lanes, tracks and fields far away from roads and houses. A responsible Boy Scout brought up the rear, closing gates after us. At last, there was our site, under high trees in a gently sloping, tree lined, grassy field. We halted alongside a patch of open ground that led directly to a wide, clear, cool stream. A metre or two upstream was a small waterfall, no more than three metres high. Skipper and the Scouts who had been there before scratched around under the bushes and pulled out a log that had been cut in half lengthways and roughly hollowed out. This log was rammed into the top of the waterfall, tied up to the trees for support and lo, there was a shower.

Skipper ordered that we all strip off. We got absolutely

starkers, with not a thread for our modesty – not that we cared. We were ordered to ford the knee-high stream, pause under the shower, then cross to the far bank and there await developments. Protestations from those of us who had no towels were met with Skipper's laconic, "Borrow one or roll on the grass".

Into the water we went – *gosh, it was cold* – under the shower we paused – *damn, it was bloody cold* – and across to the far bank we waded. The bank was narrow and not very wide. On both sides were dense trees, bushes and nettles, behind was a four-metre vertical bank, far above a full canopy of leafy branches. We crowded together wondering what would be next, when came the first of the billy cans of cold water. Fun over, we were ordered back to beg the use of a sopping towel, or roll on the grass.

It was lunch time: we could eat as soon as the billy was boiling. We were instructed to collect flat stones, sticks and small branches. The stones were used to construct a hearth, the sticks as kindling and the small branches as firewood. A Scout filled the billy can with water, put it on the fire and fiddled until he was happy that the water level was horizontal. Skipper used his hand to scoop out things that swam, wriggled and floated. Job done, it was time to hand over our tea. Paper bags of all shapes, sizes and colours were produced. I saw how difficult it was to get two teaspoons of tea out of a really big and well-creased carrier bag. Skipper cursed all through the operation. Mam had packed my tea and sugar in aluminium foil; the problem was that both tea and sugar were in the same packet. Skipper cursed me out for that.

With the billy boiling we ate our sandwiches; most of us had corned beef or cheese, or both.

"Dip your cups in the billy and don't drop your cup in," we heard.

Smarmy Scouts and smarmy Cubs dipped their cups into the can, stirred in their sugar and added milk.

Some of us did not have cups; we had not been told to bring any. We had not been told anything about cups – or towels. Protestations from those of us who had no cup were met with Skipper's laconic, "Borrow one or go without."

Sandwiches eaten and tea drunk, we were ordered to put all paper and paper bags on the remains of the fire. On future day camps I took a towel, my father's enamel shaving mug and milk and kept them to myself.

One week in the year was nationwide Bob-A-Job Week for Scouts and Cubs. In that week we were expected to tour the streets of an evening and on the Saturday, but never on the Sunday, knocking at doors to ask the occupier if they had any jobs they wanted doing for a bob. A bob was a shilling: twelve old pence, or five new pence in decimal currency. It was worth something indeed: two bars of chocolate or four portions of chips. All proceeds were meant to go to charity. We had a book for the occupier to sign and yellow stickers to give them. The latter sported a blue tick, and were to put on their front window, to show that they had participated. If a house had a sticker, we knew it was pointless going there again, for whilst people patronised us, they were only prepared to give once.

Come Bob-A-Job Week, I put a sticker in our own front window, donned my uniform and was out running, usually with Roger or Geoffrey Partridge. Sometimes Martin (Freddie) Sheldon tagged along.

Martin was not in the Cubs, nor did he have a uniform, but a bob was a bob. Family and neighbours first – they were an easy touch. Afterwards we looked farther afield, to the posh districts first, but found they were a bit on the tight side. We quickly ran to the less well-off districts, where people were cheerful, encouraging, and while not overly generous, they did give us our bob and often a drink and cake. The drill went: knock at the door, wait five seconds, knock again; *hurry up here we have money to make*. The door opened, my mouth opened and out gushed the practised spiel:

"Hello, sir (or ma'am – politeness paid), have you a Bob-A-Job for us, please, sir (or ma'am)?"

A patronising smile, a teasing pause for thought, a smile and a yes. We had to work for our money. We chopped hard logs with blunt axes, shovelled coal with rusty shovels, weeded wet gardens, moved heavy furniture, emptied dirty sheds. Not far short of slave labour, but we enjoyed it.

"Ah, how nice, nice boys, good cause, look at them, the little dears," we heard the people of the house saying about us.

Job done, we asked if they were pleased. They always were; there were smiles all around and pats on the head. We were told to wash our hands, then given a drink and a cake, before being paid our bob. With a wink and another head pat, another penny was slipped in. We gave them a sticker, explaining why very seriously, as they struggled not to smirk.

"To save you further bother, sir (or ma'am)," we said.

If they did not ask to sign the book we were quickly

out and fast away, for that bob was ours. We made ourselves a few bob in that week. We kept quiet about it, or we would have got a slap for stealing. At the Cub hut, the goody two-shoes boasted about how much they had made and smarmily handed over lots of bobs, to handshakes and applause. The rest of us jingled loose change in our pockets and discussed which picture to go and see and whether to have a fish and chip blow-out before or after the picture. We always had the blow-out before; we were always hungry for cod and chips with salt and vinegar. Besides, we knew that in the cinema we would cram up with ice cream and popcorn. We even had money over for a bus home.

Back home to, "Where you been?"

"Cubs."

"I know that, but you are very late home."

"It is end of Bob-A-Job week. We had to hand in our money, it was counted, we were told about charity and we missed the bus home."

"Oh, I will get you some food in a minute."

"I am not hungry."

"Why?" Sharp, suspicious.

"All that work I done in the week, my stomach does not feel right."

"Oh, but you are still going to school tomorrow."

"Okay."

"What's that smell?"

"What smell?"

"You smell like chips and vinegar."

"Oh that, it is from all the old junk we had to move around the Cub hut."

"Oh."

I stayed in the Cubs for two years. I finally got out by telling my parents that I needed all my evenings to study for the Eleven Plus. Study and education featured top on my parents' list of priorities, so they agreed.

When I was nine I was nicknamed Fatty: one morning at play time, my erstwhile friend, the curly haired, tending towards chubby Raymond Newman, saw me waddling towards him.

"Here comes Fatty," he said.

"Fatty, Fatty, Fatty," chanted the gang, pointing at me.

I had my back to the school building and they were in a semi-circle around me, pointing and jeering.

"I am not fat," I screamed and lunged at them, but they easily avoided me and continued with their jibes. The name stuck; everyone called me Fatty for years.

"Is Fatty in?" friends asked when they called at the house.

The teachers called me Fatty, even shopkeepers called me Fatty. I pretended to accept it, the easy way out; for me the only way out. It was hurtful, but true.

"You're not fat," I was told at home. "You're just well built; it will change."

I knew I was a lard ball though. In the bathroom mirror I saw my jowls, breasts and bulging belly. I was worried by physical training at school: forty minutes every Wednesday morning, with vaulting horses, parallel bars, big high, dangerous things. I did my best to duck out of it, to no avail. Games on a Thursday was not so bad, as it was always football. I was always in the team of left-overs and lurked away from the action, looking enthusiastic and shouting advice.

If my Granddad heard anyone call me Fatty, he took it as a personal insult.

"He's not fat," he admonished them. "You're naughty you are. Hit them, David."

For every second he gave them, I had as many minutes of taunting. For his every word, I suffered ten cutting remarks. Granddad was not overly perceptive of moods or circumstances. Neither was his father, my great grandfather Emmanuel. It reportedly took him a while to realise that his wife had done a moonlight flit, taking their five sons with her. The youngest son was my grandfather, who was nineteen years of age at the time, which leads me to think that the boys were not dragged away screaming –especially as Granddad took his organ with him. For reasons not recorded and long forgotten Emmanuel was out of favour in the family.

Paternal great-grandfather Emmanuel

Another laugh for the gang were my elocution lessons. Although I did not use slang, for we were not allowed to, Mam thought I should learn to speak "properly". She paid Miss Gibbs two guineas for ten lessons of one hour each. Every Thursday after school I visited Miss Gibbs in her terraced house in Gibbs Road, a seven-minute cycle from my house. To me it was always a dark house. We sat in the 'studio', a sparsely furnished room, on the second floor; I on a sofa behind a coffee table, Miss Gibbs prim, proper and upright in an easy chair across from me. She was a slim, short, severe woman with a lined face and dark, shoulder-length hair, always well dressed in dark clothes.

We started with my reading aloud from a book, being interrupted and corrected. The books were always from the *Famous Five* series by Enid Blyton. I thought the books were rather silly. They were unbelievable stories of four arrogant egotists and a dog, all of whom needed a good kicking, in my opinion. The show finished with my pretending to be a newsreader. I stood in front of a pretend microphone and gave my news for the week.

Mam paid out for almost a year, but Miss Gibbs' one hour a week of perfect elocution was unable to compete with the influence of the world around me the rest of the time. Finally Mam saw sense and elocution became a thing of the past.

My timidity was a drawback in my very early years. I was shy and withdrawn; I did not join in the rough and tumble and disliked playing games. On sports afternoons I was always the last one to reach the playing field and the last one to be picked for a team. I always lost the ball at the first challenge. Other pupils left the field sweating, dirty and boisterous; I left dry, clean, and solemn. In our gymnastics class there was no way I would walk the beam or roll over the bars. The only time I ran was when I thought a fight was developing, and then I ran away fast. The only recreation activity I tolerated was swimming.

Every Monday evening, my mother took me to swimming lessons at Maindee baths. Patricia and Aunt Beat often came with us. The pool was warm and only a metre deep at the deepest end. It took three months for me to take even one stroke with my feet off the bottom. For me the only pleasing thing about it was the packet of Oxo crisps and cup of Bovril as we left.

All of a sudden though, I learned to swim. I was given a certificate for twenty-five yards, one length of the training pool, and soon after a certificate for fifty yards in the big pool. This was a full-sized pool complete with high boards and it was three metres deep at the diving end. From then on, every Monday evening, Mam took me to the big pool, where I plodded up and down the lengths. I enjoyed it but it did nothing for my weight.

The last term of my last year at primary school was relaxed. The Eleven Plus exam was behind us and teachers let us read, or draw, or play quietly while they took the opportunity to prepare for the next year. In the afternoon two double-decker council buses collected the final year children from school and took us to the swimming baths. The mood was joyous for those of us who could swim. The non-swimmers were apprehensive; they had to learn, and went to the training pool.

Three of us, myself, Geoffrey and Martin Sheldon,

told Mr Jenkins, our teacher, that we could easily swim a quarter of a mile – could we please go for a certificate? Mr Jenkins was amenable and made the arrangements.

On the day, the three of us were the only ones in the pool. Thirteen and a half lengths was the required distance, without stopping, touching the side, or touching the bottom at the shallow end. Off we went. Martin finished first, Geoffrey was a length and a turn behind him, I was last.

Geoffrey was a podgy boy who became a chef. Martin was a tall, well-built, handsome boy, confident and game for anything. He lived by the nail factory, where we found jack-stars to play with. What these were I do not know – I was told they were used for cleaning pipes. We used them for playing stars, one of our favourite games. Martin joined the Royal Navy and died of cancer when I was in my first year of university. I have not seen Geoffrey, nor heard anything of him, since I was eleven.

I had my career all mapped out at primary school: I was going to be a bus driver and Patricia was going to be my conductress. Both our parents thought it a wonderful idea.

In academic matters I was bright – always within the top five – and I sailed through the Eleven Plus and went to grammar school. Once there my troubles started all over again though. I was no longer a big fish in a small pool. My primary school classmates had gone to a new comprehensive within easy walking of our house and I felt abandoned in a crowd; there were over a hundred new starters.

Saint Julian's High School was *the* grammar school in the east side of the town. It catered for five hundred boys and five hundred girls – boys one side, girls the other and never the twain shall meet in school hours. It was well equipped with a library, a tarmac play yard, a rugby pitch for the boys and a hockey pitch for the girls, cricket pitches, cricket nets and tennis courts. No expense had been spared to churn out future university students, and that is what it did with production line efficiency. The staff were carefully selected and discipline was strict, bordering on military. We wore uniforms and the masters wore gowns and even mortar boards at special occasions.

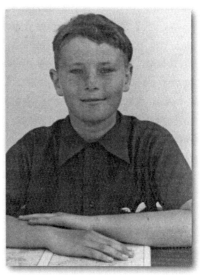

A studious boy, age 10

There were four classes (known as forms) in each year. In our first year we were allocated to a particular form by family name, all the A–F in one class, G–M in another, and so on. We were lined up in the yard and inspected every morning, before marching in step, one form at a time, into the school. This was repeated at break time and lunch time. Pity the boy who spoke, coughed, fidgeted, was not wearing his cap, or wore his tie askew. If, when unattended, we made a noise, the nearest master rushed in, selected boys at random and beat their bums with whatever he had to hand, protestations of innocence ignored.

Of a morning we waited in our classroom for our form tutor to come and take the register. There was chatter and horseplay until the door opened: instant silence, every boy standing rigid at his desk, head up, eyes straight ahead. If a boy was away from his desk, and had to pass the master to take up his position, he was given a smack on the head as he hurried by. Once the register was taken we were given news and orders for the day and marched in silence in an orderly line to the main hall for assembly, five hundred boys facing thirty masters. With the exception of a few white Catholics, all in the hall were white, Anglo-Saxon or Celtic, Protestants.

We had one class a week of religious education, except that it was really Bible study. Such a pity, the opportunity to teach us something worthwhile was missed. Mr Ponsford, the religious instructor, was a lay preacher and fan of American evangelist Billy Graham. Mr Ponsford was an extremely religious, ultra-Calvinistic yet gentle man, albeit one book short of a Bible.

"Any Catholics here?" he called between the door and desk.

A few hands went up. Reaching his desk he put down his books.

"Get out!" he ordered.

They stayed, hands still up, wondering what was going on, as we all were. Mr Ponsford turned to face the class.

"Get out, go somewhere else, you cannot take this class," was the only explanation he gave. They walked out, bemused.

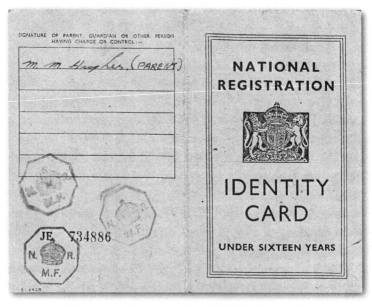

There is nothing new about UK identity cards

"Any Jews, any Jews here?" Mr Ponsford called again. No one gave an indication.

"Good," he said.

Good? Did he mean "good, that is that done" or did he mean "good, no Jews in the class"? Perhaps he meant both. I had it from men who had been through the Second World War that they did not really care about what had been done to the Jews. They did not much care for the French, Belgians and others either. These were foreigners living far away, out of sight, out of mind. They told me that they had fought because their leaders gave them no option but to fight.

Mr Ponsford had an unshakeable belief in God, Jesus, and everyone and everything in the Bible – and this included the devil. He was rabidly anti evil.

He vehemently lectured about the glorious life everlasting for the virtuous, and the fire and brimstone we were certainly heading for, if we did not quickly change our ways.

The mark of the devil and the number of the beast were real to Mr Ponsford and they were to be fought and overwhelmed. I did not believe any of it. But if there were to be a battle between good and evil, then I would throw in with Mr Ponsford. He and his fellow zealots marching off to war might actually win. They believed in themselves; no surrender and take no prisoners. The forces of evil would find Mr Ponsford a tough, determined foe.

Mr Ponsford told us how evil would start to take over the world.

"You will know this," we were told, "when it is the law that all people must have a number... and without this number you will not be able to buy things, travel, or get a job."

Further, the devil would require all our personal details to be recorded and held on file, so that our every action might be known. All good entertaining stuff to us schoolboys, but was it prophetic? Perhaps we need people like Mr Ponsford in the vanguard.

The grading of one's scholastic ability started in form one. I went down a grade every year, until I reached bottom. I just did not apply myself. I was too lazy to learn, it all seemed too much effort. An opportunity lost. It was an excellent school.

In our second year we were able to apply for the school trip to France, to help with our French. For my year the target was the village of Souillac in the Dordogne. The place and time were announced. Boys hurried to be in with their deposit, as there were only thirty places. The cost of travel from Newport to Souillac and back, full board for ten days and coach trips around the Dordogne was twenty-five pounds. I was in quickly with my deposit and was one of the thirty selected. Our parents were told to give us no more than five pounds for pocket money. On the big day we assembled at the railway station. Well groomed, dressed in our best uniform, carrying one new case filled with enough clothes to go a whole month without need for a laundry, five pounds in our wallets and much more money in other pockets. Advice from grandfathers, fathers, big brothers and uncles was fresh in our minds.

"Don't drink the water."

"The girls have diseases."

"Don't trust the Frogs."

The train took us to London for our first night. This was the big city and few of us had been there before. Granddad had told me there were strange people in London. We made it to our hotel; two, three, or more boys in a room, fighting and arguing for the top bunk.

Wash and brush up, meet downstairs and march to a restaurant for a meal.

The next day we took a train to the coast and boarded a ferry at Dover. The ferry journey was quiet, the sea was calm, and there was room and opportunity to move about. Finally I sat in the canteen drinking coffee. It was the first time I had tasted proper coffee and its flavour was as I had imagined: sweet, sharp and biting. We arrived in France in fine form and took a train to Paris, there to change to a train going south. Everyone was tired by then, and the two masters in charge of us were in a carriage somewhere, no longer patrolling the corridors to check on us. We lay on the seats, floor and luggage racks, smoking French cigarettes until we arrived.

The holiday was two weeks of new places, sights, sounds and experiences. Every day was different and it was most interesting: we saw new sights, ate different foods and talked to a different type of girl. We learned nothing and spoke only English. We drank wine and smoked. If found out the punishment was a beating.

"Do not do this; do not go there," the masters ordered. We disobeyed and revelled in our newfound freedom.

The journey back went smoothly until the boat pulled out of the harbour at Calais. Then began the worst journey of our young lives. A thirteen-year-old stomach cannot keep down any amount of wine in a heaving sea. My mate Terry Garnet was one of the few who was not sick, until an hour out, when I vomited over him. Of average height for his age, Terry had a slim build and high expectations. He was forever on the quest for a girlfriend, and worked on the principle of 'if you ask enough girls, one is bound to say yes'. Terry was bright, overly confident and willing to join in the rough and tumble and our nefarious activities. His confidence, and far away expression, gave the impression of arrogance, which did not endear him to everyone in our gang.

He joined me at the rail for the last hour, cussing me between mouthfuls. Oh, the relief at getting off. On documentaries we had seen returning soldiers kissing the ground when they disembarked... now we knew why. It felt so good not to be rocking around, stomach lurching. One disorientated boy was so relieved he took out a cigarette. The masters noticed and punishment came swiftly – with an instant beating.

Once on dry land we recovered remarkably quickly and barged our way through customs with our illicit French booze, tobacco, flick knives and pornographic magazines. We crossed London to Paddington station and a train for South Wales. It was one of those trains with a corridor on one side, so it was easy to see a master approaching. Twelve-, thirteen- and fourteen-year-old boys shared out wine and cigarettes bought on the boat. Boys were running up and down the corridor bartering, selling, borrowing. Once settled we had two hours to make ourselves sick and blame it on the travelling. Empties were thrown out of the window. Back home I gave my parents the chocolate and knick-knacks I had brought for them, and while they were distracted I hid my flick knife and pornographic magazines.

Meal tickets for the week had to be purchased first thing on a Monday morning, a shilling a meal. If, for any reason, a boy did not buy his tickets on a Monday morning he went without for the week. I sometimes brought in sandwiches: two rounds of white bread with a thick slice of Cheddar inside, another two rounds with a thick layer of corned beef inside, eaten with crisps from the tuck shop. Now that was a tasty lunch.

Some boys qualified for free meal tickets and were ordered up in front of us all.

"Who has free tickets? You boy, you do. Who else? Come on," said the master in charge.

Up they walked. At that age we were spiteful and cruel, taking the rise out of each other for just about anything. Sods we may have been, but we did not disparage these boys. Their families were poor; it was not their fault, and we all knew what being poor felt like.

In 1963, when in the fourth form, I usually had a few surplus tickets, which I sold for one shilling and two pence. No money, no ticket; I gave no credit.

At lunch time we lined up on the stairs, a master and prefect waiting at the top by the canteen door. When all was ready we filed in. The master kept order, the prefect took our tickets. The food was always warm, never hot; always bland mashed potatoes with lumps, tart green vegetables and whatever the meat for the day was. On Friday there was dried out fish. When finished we scraped our plates into a pig bin, put the dirty plates and crockery neatly in a pile and lined up for dessert, a lump of tasteless stodge, awash in watery custard.

In my O-level year, the headmaster announced in assembly that we had been disregarding the halt sign at the bottom of the hill and pedalling straight through.

"From now the police will check this and make

examples of you," he warned us.

That same afternoon at the halt sign I stopped, but did not put my feet down. I looked along the road as always: all clear, eyes front, pedal. A policeman jumped out from behind the bus shelter. There followed a court case, and I was fined ten shillings. From then on I never volunteered any assistance to the law and cheated authority in my own little way.

Come the O levels and I knew I was a no hoper. First time around I passed four papers out of the eight, but English was not one of them. I had to stay on another year to get that.

7. Childish Adventures

Farther on from Pye Corner, along the narrow lane, we reached the Severn Estuary at Goldcliff. Goldcliff dates back to about 12,000 BC, when sea levels were much lower. There is evidence there of Stone Age, Bronze Age and Iron Age cultures. Those who had sailed up the Severn saw cliffs of red sandstone speckled with mica; this is how Goldcliff was named.

At school I learned that a Norman lord, Robert de Chandos, founded Goldcliff Priory around the twelfth century. The priory was dedicated to St Mary Magdalene and was an offshoot of the abbey of Bec-Hellouin with a French prior. Said to be the richest in Wales, most of its money came from shipwrecks and smuggling. Those monks had an interesting life, praying one day and bootlegging the next; a happy bunch of reprobates. The priory was taken over by Eton College in 1462, and one day every year the Goldcliff fisheries had to send salmon to feed the college. Up until I was a young man, a working putcher rank stood in the shallows, just off Goldcliff Point; it may still be there. A putcher is a cone made of woven branches, perhaps two metres long with a hole at the narrow end and a bigger hole at the bigger end. Lots of these are put into a rack at low tide – the big end pointing upstream. At high tide the structure is submerged. Along comes Mr Salmon swimming effortlessly downstream with the tide. Mr Salmon swims into the big end without noticing. Mr Salmon's body will not go through the little end. Mr Salmon cannot turn around, Mr Salmon cannot swim backwards. Mr Salmon is buggered. Poor Mr Salmon.

On the way to Goldcliff we passed the common. All this land, from our house to the coast, was flat, not much above sea level and well serviced with drainage reens. With an exceptional high tide the reens backed up and flooded and the place stank for days. Some of the reens were up to two metres wide at water level, with clear, flowing water about thirty centimetres deep. Here, lying on the grassy bank, I sniggled for eels: I pulled a baited hook along the bottom, getting it to fall into a hole. If the eel was home and hungry I had him. I pulled the eel out, laid it on newspaper to stop it wriggling, brained it and took my hook out. The first eel I caught was cooked for me by Granny Hales, Patricia's grandmother; she was the only one who knew how. When I saw it on the plate I did not want it – it looked revolting.

The reen at the common was about one and a half metres deep and three metres across. We jumped in its cold water on hot, summer days, swallowed germs and spent the next day vomiting. Willows ran alongside all the reens. The lanes were tarred, narrow and winding. On a warm day it was an exciting place to walk, cycle, fish, and shoot rabbits with air guns. Sometimes we cycled the lanes calling at the few cottages scattered over the miles.

"Can we have your windfalls, please?" we begged.

Few refused and around the back we went to gather up apples, pears, damsons, plums and so on, from the ground. The bad ones we threw to their pigs, the good ones we took. If there were few windfalls we shook the tree. Other times we saved the bother of asking and scrumped: in through the hedge, grab handfuls, back through the hedge and cycle away laughing.

Typical reen in the Llanwern, Goldcliff, Nash area
(courtesy of Paul Flynn, MP)

Sometimes, but not very often, the farmer would be in the orchard as we passed by. The farmer sometimes, but not very often, threw a few fruit at us.

"Here lads, have an apple," he might jovially say.

His meaning was, *Now, you have your bloody apple so stay the heck out of my orchard.*

If the fruit was tart we threw it away out of sight of the farmer, so as not to hurt his feelings. If the fruit was sweet we sneaked into the orchard and scrumped a lot more of it. (Note to the farmers: it may not pay to advertise.)

The spoils were given to Mam who turned them into pies.

We were off the moors and home before evening, for it was said that strange creatures roamed the moors at night. Creatures that ran as fast as a motorbike, jumped hedgerows better than any horse, were as dark as the darkness and cried like the banshee. We enjoyed scaring each other with exaggerated tales we had heard from someone, who knew someone, who knew someone.

Every child knew the names of the wild trees, their fruit and flowers, when they budded and when they shed. The sycamore made helicopters, and there were sticky buds, acorns and conkers, ash, hazelnut, crab apple, dog rose and many more. We walked in the fields, moors and marshes, picked crab apples and rosehips, caught fledgling birds, and saw foxes, rabbits and birds of every sort. We knew there were moles about – because of the molehills seen in the parks – but we never saw one.

We chased moorhens as they dashed from hedge to water. We walked the hedgerows, looking for bird nests. We caught slow worms, *which* look like snakes but are really legless lizards. There were a lot of them under stones and piles of rubbish. Grass snakes we also caught, but not often. Common lizards were even harder to find; they were not so common. A lot of slow worms and grass snakes escaped after we had disturbed them, for we were wary of making a quick grab in case they were adders. Identity confirmed, we pounced; later we let them go. Dave Kerkland was the only one bitten by an adder. The doctor put a dressing on it and the boy was a celebrity for a week.

During the summer we caught frogs, minnows, newts and sticklebacks in local ponds, which were taken home to be neglected and die. The sun always shone and dragonflies flitted among the reeds and water plants.

A favourite countryside trick of ours was to mess about with the telephone boxes. The telephones were robust with two solid, silver buttons marked 'A' and 'B'. When the recipient answered, one pressed button 'A', the four pence dropped and the call was connected. If no one answered, one pressed button 'B' and the money dropped into the compartment at the bottom of the box. Well, it did if some child had not stuffed a rag up the chute. We stopped by now and again, pulled out the rag and shared the takings.

Sometimes we played in the avenue with our own 'telephones': two former soup or fruit cans connected by a length of string. Grown-ups told us that the string had to be pulled tight in order for it to work. So there we were, two children standing in the street pulling away from each other, one with a can to his ear, the other with a can to his mouth. Our conversation consisted of us saying:

"What?"

"You speak now."

"I can hear you."

"Did you say anything?"

"Is the string broke?"

"Course he can hear you, he's right next to you, got to be a long way away, you have, see. Go further away, but it won't work anyway," said Patricia who had rolled up intent upon spoiling things.

To go further away we had to have a long piece of string. This was difficult to find: drawers were turned out and sheds searched. Mission successful, I went into our front garden, threaded my can through the privet hedge and ducked down. My playmate did the same over the road. There we were, happily talking nonsense into cans while Patricia stood in the middle of the avenue to see fair play. Then along came a once in a morning car; it snagged our string, tore the cans out of our hands and motored up the avenue with two cans hopping and clanging behind it. We stood up, momentarily bemused, hands hurting.

"Why didn't you tell us?" we demanded of Patricia.

"Thought you would have heard the car. You could not hear each other and there is nothing else to hear. It is your own faults," Patricia stated her case.

I had a tent, a small, flimsy tent that I had never used. One day I nagged my parents to be allowed to sleep in my tent in the garden.

"You will be cold. What if it rains?" my parents had nagged back.

"I will take blankets and the forecast said no rain today," I countered. I knew nothing about any forecast, but I knew that Mam believed in such things.

"The bogey man will get you," snarled Mam, playing her ace card.

I had nagged too much to back down.

"Huh, there is no bogey man," I confidently replied, making a mental note to take my knife with me.

I whined remorselessly for another hour. Finally Dad threw my tent and sleeping bag into the garden and Mam dumped an armload of old blankets on top of it. In great excitement I erected my tent, and put an old carpet inside and blankets on top of that.

"I am sleeping outside tonight, again, in my tent, again," I bragged to my peers that evening.

I ate my supper in turmoil: had I made the right decision?

It was too late to back out now without losing face and no child wants to lose face. I went out to my tent, followed by my parents' last minute nagging. In the tent I laid my sleeping bag on top of a blanket and two blankets on top of my sleeping bag. With my shoes off I wriggled into my sleeping bag fully clothed. I heard Dad lock the back door, shortly afterwards the house lights went out. I was alone, isolated in the dark, in the back garden. I was also cold and scared of the bogey man. I zipped up my tent and double-checked that my knife was under the old coat I was using as a pillow. I did not sleep well. I was cold, I was scared and a button on my pillow had stuck in my ear. It was a long night, then came the dawn with Dad close behind. I forced myself to stop shivering and pretended to be asleep.

Gypsies, genuine Romanies, camped on the common for a few weeks of the year. We took little notice of them, their horses, or their gaudy caravans. We were wary of gypsies; they were different. They looked, sounded and acted differently to everyone else. They lived in caravans, their small horses lurking nonchalantly nearby and two or three scrawny dogs flopped under the caravans. The women often wore bright clothes and I seem to remember that all the women had big earrings.

Gypsy stories had long been told to scare children, stories warning of how gypsies would catch us and eat us, given half a chance. Less frequently, the gypsies camped on the land between the black ash path and the open sewer, a hundred metres from my grandparents' house. This was very close to where Hampden Road became Marshfield Street, at the junction of Oliver Road, with the reen-cum-open-sewer trickling under the road. The reens are now covered over and built around. I was told that the reens were declared a site of scientific interest, as eels from the Sargasso Sea return to spawn in them. Some of God's creatures have no taste at all.

Another gypsy campsite was at the end of Moorland Avenue, near our house. They were not welcome there. They were not welcome anywhere in the town and their presence was discouraged. To dissuade them further the town council issued a decree – or it may have been a 'request' – that no one was to give them water. There was no safe drinking water in the area, other than that which came from household taps. Gypsy women and children trudged from door to door with bottles and buckets, begging for water. The populace was not keen on having the gypsies nearby, but a war had just been fought so that all might have a chance in life. The council were ignored and the gypsies were given water. In truth they were no bother; they behaved, paid their way and left no mess behind them.

In 1377, Hugh, the second Earl of Stafford, granted land between Stow Hill and the River Usk shoreline to the hermits of St Augustine, known as the Austin Friars, who cared for the sick and homeless. The friars moved out of town and built an isolation hospital for contagious diseases in Lliswerry. Centuries later Spytty Park is the only memory left of this, aside from a church at West

Nash that has leper slots in the walls (through which lepers could peep and so follow the service). While I was growing up, Spytty Park was a big, clean park that was enjoyed by many people and a mere five minutes cycle from my house.

Possibly at the time of the friars Lliswerry was also known as Llebenydd, for the parishes of Goldcliff, Whitson and Nash were in the commote of Llebenydd. A commote was a secular division of land in medieval Wales. The word derives from the same root as the Welsh word for Wales, *Cymru* – comrade, countryman, compatriot, and neighbour. In Somerton there is a Libeneth Street, which runs into the old Ladyhill Quarry workings. I often wondered whether, in years gone by, this was a track leading out of Newport into Lliswerry.

We were surrounded by fields and meadows until the mid-1950s, when building work started in Green Meadow, an original name. It was to be a new housing estate; posh semis for private sale. Late one Saturday afternoon Steward, Robert and I wandered through the building site on our way back home. The building crew had finished for the day. Houses were in various stages of progress. Corona and Tizer pop bottles were scattered around, some empty, some containing dregs, others with suspicious contents, some coated in cement, some cracked, but many in prime condition. We gathered up a few to put on the wall and throw stones at.

Soon it dawned on us that there was a deposit on each bottle: three pence on Corona, four pence on Tizer. We trembled with anticipation and gathered all the bottles. We were convinced that every boy for miles around had figured it out and was heading for us. We took them to a tap, washed them and sorted out the good ones. These we took to a nearby shop. There were a lot of small shops then. With two bottles each we went in one at a time, with a respectable pause between each of us of about ten seconds. On the second round we hit grief.

"Hey, you did not buy those here. Give them me and give me my money back," proclaimed the proprietor, always an old woman.

The old crony customers in the shop were nodding and mumbling agreement. There were three of us and we stood firm outside. We felt angry – she would get the deposit off the supplier anyway. We harangued her until she gave us our two bottles back, then we walked to another shop.

We made over a shilling each that day. We dared not take it home, for if our parents had found it they would have given us a hard time, demanding to know what mischief we had been up to.

"Stealing no doubt," they would have said in supreme confidence and righteousness.

They never believed the true story. Parents never did, preferring to think we had committed a crime. We each stashed our share and promised not to spend such a big haul until it was safe. After tea we felt it was safe. We walked to town and went to the pictures. On the walk home we stopped at Selwood's chip shop, on the corner of Downing Street, and bought threepenn'orth each.

We went back to the building site every Saturday afternoon, but were not so lucky again, although we did average sixpence to nine pence each. We saved it up and every third Saturday evening we bought cod and three-penny's worth of chips, with salt and vinegar and a bottle of pop to share.

Maybe there was a penny or two left; this we hid. Do you know how difficult it is to hide a penny in a crowded house? When my parents found it there was an interrogation.

"David, we want to talk to you," they softly, always softly, said.

They call me David, while everyone else calls me Dave. I react slowly to David; it is a stranger's name, not mine.

On such occasions there was never anyone else there; my brothers had disappeared.

"We found this in your school book," they softly said.

I suppose it was a sign of guilt hiding a penny in a book, or in any equally stupid place.

"We are not angry. Say where you got it and we will say no more." Both heads nodding.

"I found a pop bottle and took it back to the shop."

"No, you didn't, you stole the penny," said together with firm, righteous insistence.

"No, it was from a pop bottle."

"Don't lie, we know you stole it. Where from?" said less softly.

"I took a pop bottle back to Prichard's."

"What pop bottle? Where did you find it?"

"Corona, Dandelion and Burdock, at the Bell House Estate."

"Aha!" said gleefully. "There is three pence back on Corona bottles. Where's the other two pence?"

"Spent it."

"What on?"

"Cod, three-penny worth, pickled egg and bottle of pop."

"That is more than two pence!" they said softly, shocked and worried.

On Mondays, on the way home from school, we called into the nearest shop.

"What do you have for a penny?" we asked.

There was always a large selection, so we tied up customers for ages, pondering and vacillating. Choice made, we left and chewed quickly, wanting to finish it before we reached home, or else:

"What are you eating, where did you get it, where did you get the money?" my parents would gabble, exhibiting a masochistic desire to prove a thief in the family.

That wasn't the end of it either.

"David, we want to talk to you," Mam and Dad said again one day, softly and in harmony.

Again my brothers were nowhere to be seen.

"Mr Richard told Mrs Gauntlet that you, Steward and Robert all spent a penny in his shop on Monday and the Monday before. Mrs Gauntlet told Mrs Thomas and Aunty Beat told me," said by my mother with a hint of so *there*!

Oh God, here we go again! I had nowhere to go; I stayed in my room with my frustration.

November brought with it Guy Fawkes Night. Miss Eriksson told us that a few hundred years ago the burning of people was not uncommon. She said that whether burned for heresy, witchcraft, or treason, some terrified soul provided family entertainment. Later, in more civilised times, or due to a shortage of victims, the effigies of villains were burned. After the 1605 Gunpowder Plot, it was the burning of Guido Fawkes' effigy that took the limelight, although Miss Eriksson told us that poor Guy was hanged, drawn and quartered on 31 January 1606. The sages told us that our bonfire originated with the old Celtic fire festival of Samhain, from the Gaelic meaning 'summer's end', which was held on the first of November. Effigies representing bad things of the year were burnt; in 1606 Guy was a prime candidate.

Something else the Christians stole: they changed it to Hallowmas, or All Saints' Day, to commemorate the souls of the blessed. The night before became known as All Hallow's Eve. I think bonfire probably came from 'bone fire', a pagan festival held during the summer. It was celebrated by burning the bones of livestock slaughtered during the past year. It was a malodorous festival, but before the days of showers and deodorants no one would have noticed.

We did not care; Bonfire Night was an event. Every November we – Patricia, me, maybe one of my brothers and whoever else was willing – made a Guy. I needed help to make the Guy, but not to collect the money. I made sure I contributed something and had the Guy made in my garden. Once finished, I started an argument to drive the others away. Sometimes, if they negotiated correctly – "I will take my dad's coat back" or "I will hit you" – they were on board with us to collect the money. Next we lugged the Guy to the bus stop at the top of our avenue, where we waited expectantly, begging all who passed by to "give us a penny for the Guy".

Once Patricia's grandmother, Granny Hales, said our Guy was the best she had ever seen and gave us a penny.

There were five of us, and together we collected about eleven pence; a respectable haul for a few hours' work. We shared the take, two pence each and a penny in the kitty. On the few metres walk home Patricia insisted I give her the penny that her gran had given us. She recognised it, as it was a shiny penny. I asked why.

"'Cos my gran gave it to us; it is mine," she said.

"But, we all have the same number of pennies." I did not know what else to say!

"I want my gran's penny," she was getting ready to bawl.

"Okay, but I want the penny my Mam gave us." Me taking a chance.

"Okay, who's got it?" Patricia spoiling things again.

Darned if I knew. Patricia bawled and went to the court of appeal, her dad. Uncle Harry called on my mum. All the collectors were rounded up and a screaming, slanging match ensued among us. Finally, the grown-ups understood and Uncle Harry explained to Patricia. No good, she wanted *that* penny.

"Okay, swap it for one of yours." Me at the end of my tether.

No way! Bawling, tears, ranting... she wanted her gran's penny *and* the ones she already had.

Two weeks before Bonfire Night we started to scavenge burnables for our bonfire; even Dad helped. We hunted far and wide: fallen branches from the hedgerows, sticks and logs stolen from the allotment, bits of wood pulled through the fence of Tanner's wood yard. With this we built a small fire in the back garden. On the big night Dad ushered everyone back and lit the fire to start the festivities. A lot of matches, a bit of swearing and an exhibition of bad temper marked the lighting of our fire, better than any Lord Mayor's speech. Fire lit, we all moved forward, then the fire went out. Dad called for more paper and matches and went in again striking matches, blowing and fanning. With the fire going Dad rushed to the kitchen to hold his fingers under the cold water tap, while hopping from foot to foot. Mam used a long stick to push a few big potatoes into the fire to bake. The potatoes always burnt to a cinder, but we had to eat them. We pretended they were delicious. Sometimes Granddad visited, other times we went to Patricia's; Uncle Harry always had a big fire that he started quietly with one match.

Uncle Harry was not a blood uncle, nor was his wife, Aunty Beat, my real aunt. In Wales in those days, children called close neighbours and family friends 'uncle' and 'aunty'. Uncle Harry kept chickens until I went to high school. He knocked one off now and again, but did not let us watch. He had three apple trees and some other fruit trees in the garden, which gave us shade and places to hide.

Grandfather Hales had bought their house many years before, for three hundred and sixty pounds, my father told me. When Uncle Harry married Aunty Beat, they moved in. Grandfather Hales died first, then Aunty Maggie (Grandma Hales's sister) went and Grandma Hales lasted a few years longer. She was once a nursing assistant. If anyone was hurt, or ill, in our end of the street, then Grandma Hales was sent for. Along she tottered, a short, plump, round-faced, kind old lady. I always liked Grandma Hales.

In these years, my mother tried hard to make me play with my next brother down, Geoffrey. She was very cross when I refused, and so were my grandparents, aunties and neighbours.

"Why don't you play with your little brother?" whinged and quavered parents, grandparents, aunties and neighbours. "Take him out with you, David, don't be a bad boy."

And the irritating, "He's little, like you!"

He was almost four years younger than I was. In my childhood years, those four years were half a lifetime, and we had nothing in common. So I left him to find his own age group. The grown-ups never fathomed this. They did not understand that a four-year age gap is nothing when both are over twenty. When pre-teen though, a four-year gap is socially unworkable. It was hell for my peace of mind, all that nagging from family and neighbours and the feeling of guilt.

A local character was Sammy the rag-and-bone man. Thursday was the day for his weekly scavenge. He arrived in the avenue, sitting sideways on his flat cart geeing on a shambling horse. He swapped goldfish, tortoises or trinkets for handfuls of soiled rags. The rag quality was vetted and the rubbish ones thrown back at us. The quantity was assessed and if insufficient, all was thrown back. The child was bidden to ask his mam for more. This was difficult: every rag was worn until it frayed, then used for cleaning shoes and then floors. It did not take many rags to earn a fish or two, but a tortoise demanded a big armful. Nonetheless, every child had one: the poor creatures were kept in the yard, eating garden grass. If lucky they lived a month or two.

One thing I still do not know: what the heck did Sammy do with the rags? Why did he not ask for bones? At one time Gran kept a pile of ash in the garden.

"In case the ash man calls again," she explained. I knew ash was used in soap making.

Sammy only had one leg, a sallow complexion, a hunch and squinty eyes. He slurred his words and dressed in rags. He was a bit of a mess, although a fitting advert for his trade. We mocked him, not from close by but from the safety of distance, for he used his crutch at close quarters. Grown-ups treated Sammy with more respect.

"He was not always like that," said those who had known him a long time ago. They said he was once a pleasant boy; not tall or handsome or particularly bright, but not bad looking.

When talking of Sammy, adults mentioned the First World War, the disasters and the waste, the shell that took his comrades and his leg. I much later realised that the war took his mind as well.

In the 1950s young men still did national service and were cheered off by those who had been before them. At the station, on the way to their barracks, they were treated like heroes and bought cups of tea, yet they had never been to war. Their elder brothers had done the fighting. Now, some few years later, the elder brothers walked quietly, said little, made no fuss or bother and gave Sammy a nod and a penny now and then. Some resembled Sammy as they hobbled along. Their one-time comrades, whole and hearty, were embarrassed to look them in the eye. For us children the Somme was a place that was simply too far to walk. Sammy stopped coming; no one said why. Maybe his horse died.

When we had lived with my grandparents the ice cream man had been Nocivelli. To us he was 'Knocker'. Old man Knocker delivered ice cream down Gran's street in his horse-drawn cart. The cart was very high; it was a tiptoe job to get my pennies on the counter and then only if he was near the kerb. If he parked away from the kerb there was no way I was able to reach, and from where he lounged there was no way he could see me. Maybe he saw a hand waving, or the top of a head bobbing up and down, but he ignored me. I asked my grandparents or my parents to buy for me, but was told to do it myself. I sometimes went without, but no worry, his ice cream was bland and gritty. Most ice cream and confectionery then was poor tasting, but it was all we had. The cart was a basic clean white, with broad, red, vertical stripes. It had a sloping roof canopy, the paintwork of which matched the main body work. Old man Knocker was interned during the war; being Italian he was considered an enemy citizen. It was said that he spent the war years writing letters to his sons, who were serving with the South Wales Borderers.

A few years later, the ice cream man was Knocker junior, the old man's son. He was advanced in his trade: he had a motorised van, a cube-shaped vehicle, off-white and blue in colour. His ice cream was as bad as his father's. He made blocks of ice cream, with or without a thin, watery chocolate layer.

"Sixpenny off the block, Knock," we requested in our later years, when affluent.

Other horse and cart deliverers included the bread man, the grocer, the milkman and the coal man. The coal man, Mr Wesson, owned his own business. His granddaughter, Lorna, was much later to marry Lyndon Smith, who I met in my teens. Lyndon was two years older than I was, one-point-nine metres tall and one hundred and forty kilograms on a light day. Lorna was one-point-seven metres tall and a hundred kilograms any day. I was best man at the wedding.

Our milk was delivered by the Huish family; at that time most milk came in glass bottles with foil tops. Huish also owned one of the local fish and chip shops. Later they expanded and sold chocolate, cigarettes and other small profit, high turnover goods. Huish were the first to put a milk vending machine outside their shop. The machine was light blue, maybe one-point-eight metres high, almost a metre wide and perhaps six hundred millimetres deep. For sixpence there was a choice of plain, strawberry or banana milk. Maybe half a litre, in a waxy container, with a perforated circle to poke out to get at the liquid. It was probably carcinogenic, but it tasted lovely to a youngster. Strawberry was by far the best, banana a close second. I saw no reason to buy plain milk. At night, when the shop was long closed and all was dark and quiet, I put in my sixpence. As I pressed the strawberry button, just at the right time, I kicked the machine hard at the bottom, just in the right place. Nine times out of ten I had the satisfaction of hearing two cartons tumbling down. Occasionally, just very occasionally, three.

Every Saturday morning the Corona soda-pop truck trundled into our avenue. Every week we had four bottles of one-litre soda pop between us. Having four bottles allowed us to have, on loan, our own wooden bottle crate. The four bottles we chose were lemonade, an orange-coloured, vaguely orange tasting soda, an apple-flavoured soda and my favourite, dandelion and burdock. Occasionally we alternated one of our flavours for a red-coloured soda that was reputed to be raspberry flavour. Mam rationed out the pop to see us through the week; it was doled out ad hoc for no apparent reason. Being thirsty did not help.

"Mam, I'm thirsty," always brought the response "Water's in the tap."

We often had lemonade powder somewhere in the house; in desperation we made our own drink, but it was never the same, not even close.

Every Sunday morning and sometimes on the odd weekday evening, the Wall's ice cream van trundled into our avenue. Wall's did not get much business from us on a weekday evening though. He came too late and Knocker beat him. Sunday morning was when he received our custom.

"Wall's is here, the ice cream man is here, it's Wall's, ice cream, Wall's is here, quick, quick, it's Wall's, can we have ice cream? Wall's is here, can we have a block, can we, can we? Quick, Wall's is here," children ran home screaming.

My parents gave me one shilling and three pence to buy a block and out I ran. The block was usually vanilla but sometimes vanilla and strawberry. Our ice cream was limited to vanilla, strawberry, chocolate and a pleasing green colour, the name of which I have forgotten. Coffee flavoured ice cream popped up here and there. Later

Wall's gave us tutti-frutti, banana and pineapple, which were exciting and very popular. Mam wrapped the block in sheets of newspaper and put it in a cold place in the pantry. It was eaten after Sunday lunch and was often still firm. The newspaper insulation worked. When we slept in our tents, we placed crumpled newspaper under our sleeping bags for insulation.

While I was still in primary school Wall's had started selling ice cream cakes. These were a big hit for birthday parties. Come the evening of my birthday and all my mates were at my house, then Wall's pitched up at just the right time. The pre-ordered, pre-paid for cake was collected and put, rock hard, on the table. A sharp knife and muscle were used to make holes in it. Candle holders were hammered in. Candles were inserted into the precariously balanced holders and lit. Everyone was compelled to sing *Happy Birthday* as I blew out the candles. Compulsory singing finished, we waited for a slice of cake. Could Mam cut it? She could not! That cake was rock hard. Knives bent, sweat dribbled, yet only small shavings flaked off. We were ordered to go and play for a while. This we did, keeping the cake in sight at all times.

"Is it ready yet?" we asked Mam every five seconds.

The cake was hard because it had not long come out of a freezer. Further, to keep it cold, lumps of dry ice (carbon dioxide) were put into the box with the cake. The sublimation point of carbon dioxide at atmospheric pressure is about minus seventy-eight degrees Celsius, yet children were allowed to play with it! I put it in water to see the water bubble and foam and then drank the cold water. No one knew that to swallow a piece of dry ice was to risk injury.

Our avenue saw its fair share of horse traffic and now and again one of them made a pile. By tradition it went to the family who lived in the nearest house, but many housewives appeared with shovels, waiting for the cart to move on. With the cart gone they sauntered to the pile, feigning surprise when appearing to notice the competition. Then they set to, just like a hockey bully-off.

If the horse unloaded within discreet range of the house, they edged toward the gate with buckets and spades. If the horse did it too far away, it was undignified to go for it – although some hussies did run down the street with their buckets and spades, like children on the beach. When the horse was within the psychological range of a few houses, the housewives sauntered towards utensils and gate, looking everywhere except at the pile.

"Oh, look, just what my husband wanted; lucky the shovel and bucket were in the front garden," they said, once clear of their gate.

All walked forward as if to inspect; then they pounced, pretending not to fight for it. The winner walked home with as much dignity as could be mustered by someone carrying shit in a bucket.

Not all merchants cruised the byways in horse-drawn carts and motorised vehicles. Some walked, others cycled. The Wall's ice cream vendor sometimes patrolled the streets on his customised tricycle, with the famous sign prominent at the front: 'Stop Me And Buy One' (a slogan that was later re-arranged for condom vending machines as 'Buy Me And Stop One'). We had the knife sharpeners and general tinkers, cycling on their unstable contraptions or pushing their carts. The brush salesmen walked from door to door – a soul-destroying job.

Photographers blitzed the district with slick, quick patter, persuading housewives to record the images of their nearest and dearest for posterity, before the little doves left the nest. We only once had a French onion seller, and he was as surprised as we were. But these vendors very rarely, if ever, left a deposit in the street. They were no good for the roses.

In my last years of primary school, construction of the Llanwern Steelworks began, on the moorland between Lliswerry and Llanwern. This was marsh ground, and when it was wet anything heavy sank into it. Llanwern means 'the church on marshy ground'. It was a small village on the edge of the Caldicot Levels – land reclaimed from the sea by ancient Roman engineers who exploited a nearby salt marsh. Much later, monks from Goldcliff Priory dug a drainage ditch from Wentwood to the Bristol Channel to reduce the threat of flooding. It did not help much, for the Great Flood of 1606-7 breached the sea defences, reaching depths of over a metre inland.

The whole steelworks, buildings and roads, needed foundations. The start was to lay shale, pieces of rock. This was mined in the valleys and bought to Llanwern by lorry. The shale lorries operated on piece-work: they were paid by the load. Everyone who had the money bought a lorry and hired a driver. All day, all night, nose to tail, these heavy beasts moved through Newport, passing our quiet avenue and continuing into the marsh land. The more loads, the more money; the drivers stopped for nothing. They worked long hours, their vehicles were not cared for, and traffic regulations went by the board. Cars were not able to leave the avenue – the lorries did not stop, nor leave space. Buses were unable to get through either, with loaded lorries going one way, empty lorries speeding the other. Parked cars were shunted, garden walls driven down, trees run over, children and prams forced hard against walls. Horns blaring, lights flashing, tired drivers screamed obscenities and drove on. If flagged down they simply refused to stop. If issued with a ticket they ripped it up. No serious action was taken against any driver, nor any owner. Hundreds of lorries nose to tail in both directions. They choked the town for over a year. Rates were increased to pay for road repairs. When I was older I realised that money talked. It was criminal. What happened over that period showed the utmost contempt for the people who lived there.

8. Summer Holidays and Other Treats

One of the big adventures of those days was to take the side paddle steamer from Clarence Place wharf to Weston-super-Mare. It was operated by the White Funnel Fleet and ran according to the tide. We chugged down the Usk past the docks, out into the Severn Estuary, turned right and plodded along. The voyage did not take long and the estuary was rarely rough. We viewed the engine room from a visitor's walkway. While the grown-ups sat or stood in the bar, children wandered around. No one kept an eye on us; any one of us could have gone over the side. Water clearance, I noted, was not much, not even half a metre. I did not fancy the boat's chances in an open sea.

The wharf at Weston was on the seafront. We moored at the narrow pier, and were told what time to return. Then we barged ashore and split up to do what we each wanted to do. I ran straight to the amusement arcade. There I changed my half-crown into pennies, thirty of them, and played the slot machines, trying to win cigarettes and chocolate. Ten minutes in the amusement arcade: all my money gone and nothing won. I hunted down my parents and waited, bored, for the trip back.

The biggest bind of the day was the bus ride home in the evening. The ride was not so bad; it was the wait that annoyed me. If we had just missed a bus, the twenty-minute wait for the next was a long time for a young boy to stand around, especially in the company of tired parents.

Barry Island is a seaside resort in the Vale of Glamorgan. It is a quiet part of the coast today, but it was once a true island, and the private domain of smuggler Thomas Knight, who fortified the shoreline and operated a fleet of smuggling ships from there. It was high on our agenda of 'nearby places to visit when the children are playing up'.

We took a bus to town and a train to Cardiff, where we changed trains. At Barry station we walked across the road to the seafront and changed on the beach with towels protecting our modesty. We splashed in the sea, ate boiled eggs, cheese sandwiches and crisps, drank warm tea from a thermos and hung around for a while. Finally, what we had really come for: the fairground. Very occasionally we went to Porthcawl, usually for evening fireworks, whose fairground was noticeably better.

It was better to go with others as then I had more adults to make a fuss of me or friends with whom to play and explore. If I went with my grandparents I was spoilt rotten and wanted for nothing, and they bought fish and chips to eat on the train coming back. They also took buckets with them and harvested cockles and whelks from the sea. The full buckets were lugged back on the train and carried home in triumph.

Once Raymond Newman, the initiator of my nickname Fatty, had his mam take him and me to Barry. That was a delightful day. Egging each other on we dropped pebbles from the promenade onto people on the beach below and smeared ice cream onto seats. Raymond's mother vowed never to take us anywhere, ever again.

For summer holidays we went to resorts on the south coast of England and to Blackpool on a few occasions. The holiday business was stressful for my parents. A week in advance they made a list of all that needed to be taken and a lot more that did not need to be taken. The list was revised every evening in deep consultation. Departure day minus one, Mam took everything on the list and laid it out in the front room.

"That shirt is supposed to go with!" Mam panicked.

Nothing for it but to take it off me, then quick hand wash, wring well, iron wet and lay out to dry overnight.

On departure day we cleaned our teeth quickly and put our toothbrushes on the pile. Mam folded everything up and packed it. If all did not go in the chosen cases, then Dad was up into the attic, or out to the shed, for other cases, considering the best combination. He checked the windows were closed and curtains drawn. The door was closed and shaken to check and the house key was dropped off with Aunty Beat – Mam all the time asking if we had everything. We walked to the bus stop, Dad carrying the heavy case, Mam carrying one not so heavy, I and whichever brothers could walk carrying bags, buckets and spades. We looked like refugees.

On the bus we packed everything under the stairs and sat on the lower deck to keep an eye on our stuff. Once in town it was a short hobble to the railway station, frequently stopping to change hands. At the station Dad bought our tickets. We crushed through the turnstile and staggered to the platform, Dad having asked at least three porters which platform it was. There we waited at least half an hour for the train, double-checking with three more porters, or perhaps the same ones, if this was the right platform.

"Waaa laade waaa do di dah," came the station announcement.

"What did he say, Bill?"

"I don't know, Marge."

They looked enquiringly at others on the platform. Dozens of heads shook in unison.

Ever helpful I said, "He said, 'Waaa laade waaa do di dah'."

God, the look again! Two pairs of eyes seared into my soul and wished me death.

The train chuffed in and stopped with a wheeze. All pretended to stand back while really pushing and barging. We were on, but we were scattered and our belongings were more scattered than we were. All the way Dad patrolled the corridors, keeping an eye on our luggage. We reached the station where we had to change trains – one hell of a scramble to collect our stuff and get out. Off the train, dump something, back on the train for more. Dad held the door open while Mam checked we had everything. Loaded up, we were off to catch the next train, Dad asking every railway worker we passed for the right platform. At the platform we had another half-hour wait. We reached our destination; now to find the boarding house. We started walking.

"Only three minutes from the station," the landlady's letter had said. We found the place, collectively gasped and stood back with our mouths open.

"It will be nice inside," said Mam.

Blackpool – there was a place! Crowds of noisy people hustled and bustled along the beachfront, entertainment events were advertised everywhere and there was the famous Blackpool Tower. We got to the tower early in the morning, while it was quiet. First I took the lift up to the top. I did not want to, but I had to: I did not want my school friends to know that I was scared. Squeezed inside the small iron cage I was rattled and shaken, then up and up and up we went. I tried not to look down, but was drawn to do so. It was a long, frightening journey to the top. I stepped out onto the platform and into the rain or shine. I went straight to a handrail where I feigned interest in the view. I held the handrail tightly and forced myself to look out, down and over the town. Stepping back, still clinging to the handrail, and with my eyes only on things at my level, I feigned nonchalance as I groped around to the telescope. I put my coin into the slot and quickly scanned the sea, coast and town before my money ran out. I descended with a happy heart.

"Ha! I went up to the top of the tower," I could tell the gang. "Nothing to it. I stayed up ages and had a good look down."

I experienced my first aeroplane flight at Blackpool, a trip around the tower; it was expensive at a few shillings per person. The plane, I was told, was a converted wartime craft. The pilots were two bored-looking young men who sold tickets, hand-pumped fuel into the wing tanks, and then collected tickets. I boarded the plane in anticipation. The pilot asked that all children sit on the lap of a parent, as there were not enough seats. As the plane started down the runway, my excitement grew to unprecedented levels.

The pilot asked that those who did not have a seat and who were standing in the aisle, please sit on the floor. The plane staggered upwards and banked as I looked out of the window. The ground was so far below, people and cars looked minute. It was worse than being up Blackpool Tower. There was no rail to hold on to and I could not go down when I chose. I could not close my eyes either as Dad expected me to look, and look eager. My excitement vanished, to be replaced by anxiety. Sod flying. I wanted to get off.

My maternal grandmother (Nana Knight), brother Geoffrey, Mam and me at Blackpool

We went to the beach every day that it was not raining – this was why we took holidays at the seaside. The cost of a day at the beach was the rental of two deck chairs. It was frowned upon not to rent a deck chair, unless one was posh and had both a beach umbrella and a blow up mattress, then called a lilo. Children did not have deck chairs; children sat on the sand.

We arrived at the beach early to stake out a prime space, rented our chairs and threaded through the gathering throng. Once we had spotted a prime site near the ocean, we made a nonchalant, straight line gallop over other people's towels to the site, pitched the deck chairs and spread our things out to occupy as much space as possible. Settled, we realised the site was empty because the tide was coming in. We decamped and walked back red-faced through amused settlers to high ground. There we walked along the beach past smirking faces, until we reached a place where no one smirked, and walked a ways after this.

"Oh, much better down here it is, I remember now," said Dad. He had not been there before.

We pitched camp again, hemmed in by others, the sea visible through myriad deck chairs and beach accoutrements. The neighbouring men folk, like Dad, were dressed in shirt, tie, trousers and smart shoes. Some wore suits. A lot wore caps or hats. Anyone wearing casual clothes was pointedly stared at and talked about. I wore a shirt and tie, smart shorts and my school shoes.

"David, would you like a donkey ride?" Mam wheedled on our first day on the beach.

I had known this was coming.

"No."

"You do!"

"I don't."

"You'll like it," Mam countered with fraying patience.

"I won't."

"You will, you know you will," said Mam with more than a hint of anger.

"I don't like it. I don't want to," I whinged, feeling cornered.

"You do," she replied decisively. "There's an empty donkey there, take him over, Bill."

Dad dragged me away.

"I don't want to," I shouted.

"Go on, you do!"

Finally, I steeled myself, got on the donkey, wrapped the reins around my hands, grabbed the saddle horn in death grip and clamped my knees so tightly that the donkey's legs buckled. I closed my eyes and waited. We were off, jog, jog, jog along the beach, Dad trying to focus his camera while yelling at me to open my eyes. My eyes stayed closed and my legs tightened round the donkey, which was gasping for breath and falling behind the herd. Back at the start line I was lifted off, the donkey grunted. I unwrapped the reins from my hands and the blood flow restarted with a tingle. My feet touched the ground and I opened my eyes.

"Did you like that?" Dad asked me boisterously.

"No."

"Oh, you did."

We arrived back at our site.

"He liked that, Marge."

"Knew he would."

Later another annoyance: the Punch and Judy man arrived. He set up on the sand as best as he could in the crush and breeze. He had drunk a few beers and he dropped things and fell over a lot when bending to pick them up. He was nearby, but not too near. I wished him miles away.

"You can see better from over there, David," Mam

piped up. "Take this sixpence with you to pay him after."

"I don't want to see it."

"You do!"

"I don't."

"You will like it."

"I won't."

"You will, you know you will."

"I don't like it, I don't want to."

"You do," Mam insisted. "There is a place to sit there, take him over, Bill."

"I don't want to."

"Go on, you do!"

Other children were laughing, but not me. It was the same old plot every time. I put my mind in neutral, while sitting on sand surrounded by, I thought, morons. Show over. *Hallelujah*! The wizened reprobate walked around for his sixpences. Most of the children paid up – the clever ones had already run off to the ice cream man. The Punch and Judy man now walked around the deck chairs, hassling adults for sixpence.

"You seen the show, you must pay!" he accused.

"We did not want to see it. You pitched your stall by us and bored us stupid for twenty minutes!"

"Never mind, you seen it, you must pay!"

"Ah, bugger off, you bloody old fool." This came from the women.

The bloody old fool buggered off. I started to walk back to our site, but after two steps I was lost. Dad came towards me.

"Did you like that?" he asked me boisterously.

"No."

"Oh, you did."

We arrived back at our site.

"He liked that, Marge."

"Knew he would."

From eleven-thirty onwards people reached into their bags for food. Out came sandwiches, crisps, cakes, thermos, and soda pop. One or two 'right lads' had a bottle of ale. Giggling, they popped the top and the bottle was quickly up to the mouth as warm froth oozed out. They drank to sniggers and side glances from others. We sat in the middle of chomps, slurps, burps and egg smells.

We were staying in lodgings, so we did not have sandwiches or thermos. We waited until twelve-thirty, returned the deck chairs and quick-marched to our digs for a lunch of soup followed by meat and two veg. It was the first time I had eaten soup, which was thought to be for posh people – and we did not want to appear pretentious. I looked around to see how other people were dealing with the soup, Mam and Dad were doing the same. Trying not to smirk I went for it.

"Don't spill it, be careful, don't slurp," Mam and Dad hissed at me.

The soup finished, the main course arrived and, by gosh, what a surprise: it was so much better than anything Mam had ever made.

Years later we bought a lilo, just the one between all of us, so we took it in turns to lie on it. As soon as we had unpacked Dad blew it up, hyperventilated and keeled over.

Before the end of our stay we had to buy traditional seaside rock, a stick each for the children at home. We never bought the tasty humbug, pineapple or strawberry;

always that hateful red stuff. I was given the same by others who came back from holiday.

"Say thank you, David," Mam would say.

"Thank you," said I.

Later I said, "Mam, I don't like this rock."

"Eat it. Mrs Jones brought it all this way for you."

On the second day there we had to buy postcards for everyone we knew, and write and mail them that day.

"Else," Mam said, "we will be home before they arrive."

The choosing of the postcards was an event in itself: scenic for neighbours and friends, ribald ones for family.

"What do you think of this for Mrs Jones, Bill?"

"Nice, Marge."

"And this for Mrs Thomas?"

"Nice, Marge."

"How about this for your mam?"

"Nice, Marge."

Anguish: they had found three attractive cards but they needed another two dozen.

"If you like that one so much, why not buy a dozen of them?" I tried to help.

"David, how can we send the same card to twelve people?"

"Easy! They do not know each other, live tens of miles apart and are not likely to ever meet each other, let alone compare your holiday postcard, which they will throw away less than ten days from now."

I thought I made sense, but I did not win support for my scheme. The same saga ensued for the writing of the message on the back. They agonised for hours.

"Tell Gran about such and such," I helpfully suggested.

"Already told Mrs Phillips that," said Mam, sounding despondent.

"But they do not know each other, live a hundred miles apart and are not likely to ever meet each other, let alone compare your holiday postcard, which they will throw away less than ten days from now."

Again I got the pitying look. I neither sent postcards, nor bought rock.

In the spring and summer the Billy Smart and Chipperfield's circuses came to Newport. Sometimes they sneaked in quietly and set up camp at Shaftsbury Park. Other times they offloaded at the railway station and paraded through town to Shaftsbury Park, where pavements both sides of the road thronged with people. There were horses obediently trotting along and elephants, each with a mahout. Big cats in cages came next, clowns, jugglers, acrobats, 'cowboys and Indians' on horseback followed up – everything everyone expected from a proper circus, all done up in their circus clothes. The cowboys and Indians had all the gear. They carried rifles just like we saw in the cowboy pictures. These they fired into the air, littering the road behind them with discharged cartridges. Children braved the horses' hooves to grab them.

The night of the circus was a big event. First a walk to the bus stop to catch the number six: I stood on the corner watching for the bus to come over the level crossing, and when it was in sight I ran to the bus stop.

"It's coming!" I screamed.

At the terminal we caught a bus going Malpas way, and then came another walk. The disappointment was the long queue, because I hated queuing. Everyone was excited, regardless of age. Finally we were in. We felt obliged to buy an expensive, but needless, glossy programme.

After a tedious wait, the lights dimmed, and in strode the ringmaster to open proceedings in a strident voice. The band struck up *March of the Gladiators*, all the acts trooped in, and paraded around the ring and out again. Children and old folk cooed at the animals and laughed at the clowns. The men ogled the well-built female acrobats, the younger men whistled and catcalled.

Then at last we were off, lost to the world for what seemed a very quick two hours. At the end of the show everyone rushed for the exit before the national anthem was played.

If we were not quick off the mark we were battered by the flow. Some people stood for the national anthem, but they were a sad minority; the Hughes family was up and running. Around us, mothers ran holding their babies and toddlers were pulled along by their fathers.

Once a year a funfair came to Lliswerry too, though it was a fairly mundane affair. It was a tatty outfit that set up on the land between the black ash path and the open sewer, a hundred metres or so from my grandparents' place, at the site used by the Gypsies. Granddad liked the amusements, but not the rides. He insisted I wanted to go and he did not mind taking me. On the walk there he always told me that he wanted to roll the cartwheel two-penny piece. Old cartwheel coins were rolled down a slide and if they landed inside a tight square without touching the lines, we won what was written in the square. Granddad never won anything.

I was only allowed on the rides if a parent was with me. I was a timid child: I wanted to go on the rides, yet I did not want to. I did ride the dodgem with my mother though, and I often banged my face on the steering wheel. Everything stopped while I was helped out crying, blood dribbling from my nose.

In the 1950s, we had six cinemas in town. Up until the age of nine or ten, I often went to the Saturday morning children's cinema. It was sixpence well spent: a cartoon, a comedy, the serial, news and the big film. Unfortunately, there was a compulsory sing-along halfway through. A junior member of staff was shoved onto the stage and tried to lead us through *On The Good Ship Lollipop* and other songs. For this they turned on the lights, to see who was throwing what at the poor lad. We took stones and cans in with us, especially for this. It was dangerous on that stage; we had no conscience or respect.

Aunty May and Uncle Charles; photographs taken just before the Second World War

Sometimes, on Saturday afternoons, I visited the cinema with my cousins, Leslie and Charlie, twin boys. They were the sons of Dad's twin sister, my Aunty May, a kindly, chubby lady. Their father, Charles Sellick, had been killed in a North African campaign before they were born. The twins were four years older than I was, but they let me tag along when they went places. To me they were 'big boys', my role models.

On the walk back from the cinema we stopped at a chemist's shop, to buy a long liquorice root for a penny. Like sweet shops, the chemist had rows of glass bottles, with black, screw-on caps that held all sorts of wonderful things. They sold Victory Vs that burnt my tongue.

The twins and their mam lived with Granddad's brothers, Uncle Bill and Uncle Sam, in Gaskell Street, a hundred metres in a straight line from 'The Chem', a chemical works on Corporation Road. It rendered animal bones to make glue. Frequently an incident within the factory allowed the product to escape containment. The stench was foul, akin to rotting meat. There was a park right in front of the factory. In my childhood days Gaskell Street was a short cul-de-sac; entry was from Corporation Road. The other end was blocked off by black, corrugated sheets. In my father's day there was a wharf at the end of Gaskell Street that reached out into the Usk. Ships moored at the wharf to unload sand at the now long-gone Sessions Sand Distributors. Dad often saw lascar seamen walking, single-file and barefoot in the gutter, to the end of Gaskell Street and along Corporation Road to Coronation Park. There they sat on the grass and watched the games of football being played. It cost them nothing and it passed the time. On the other side of the Usk, opposite the wharf, there was Cashmore's, a breaker's yard, which recycled warships and civil vessels. Cashmore's operated until I was a boy. Uncle Bill was a watchman there; he let the twins and their gang into the yard on the odd Saturday afternoon, to run over the ships.

Cinema, circus, pantomime were one thing, but for real spontaneous entertainment, nothing could compare with the conveying systems for cash in the big stores. There was the suction tube that carried a cylinder and the more spectacular hanging canister that travelled suspended from a wire. When in a large store, children slipped free of adults and converged where the action was. A crowd of children stood silently, gawping and eyes fixed as the saleslady loaded the conveyer. It was triggered by a switch and away it went in a tube, with a subdued whoosh or it was triggered by pulling a cord and away it went, hanging on wheels, with a whirr and a rattle. Whichever the method it was accompanied by our chorus of "whoooooooooo".

Then we were off to find another saleslady who looked like she might soon load and launch.

Another of our pastimes was swapping cigarette cards. I remember that a Gallagher was worth two of any other. In early 1940 production of cards had ceased because of wartime restrictions and never fully resumed. Brooke Bond tea took over the role, putting cards inside their tea packets. There were fifty cards in a 'set' and I had many interesting sets. I do not know what happened to them; they just vanished. At school we flicked our cards against a wall, from a distance of about two metres. Whoever was closest to the wall after an agreed number of flicks won all the cards. I did not play this game, neither did I play marbles, for one simple reason: I disliked losing. I am a bad loser. I am an even worse winner though – I gloat and mock.

We also played knock-up-ginger in Newport: we took it in turns to walk quietly up the path, knock on a door or press a bell (our favourite), and run. We only had to run fifty metres and we were out of sight, or out of psychological range for chasing. Occasionally, though, joy of joys, we hit the jackpot when some no-hoper chased after us. We ran like whippets. When illuminated doorbells appeared, with their chiming ding-dong, we were overjoyed. We targeted these. Now and again there was a tricky gate, either spring loaded or prone to closing by itself. One of us held it open, while another did the business. Often, when the ringer turned for his home run, we closed the gate on him, leaving him trapped. It was difficult to run while laughing uproariously, the ringer's wails of despair receding with distance.

When we got home Mam knew all about it, or had a fair idea.

"You been knocking doors and running away?"

"No."

If she could prove we had done it, punishment was swift and accurate – no messing, no appeal, just whoppo. Complain, cry or shout and a few more clouts followed in rapid succession. It also made us intolerant of the whinging, do nothing, ill-disciplined children of later years.

9. Adolescence in Gwent

At home on a hot summer day, my brothers and I only broke off playing when forced to by extreme thirst. We ran into the kitchen, filled a cup with water and quaffed it.

"Don't gulp water. Sit at the table and sip it slowly!" we heard.

My parents, their parents and both their generations had traits and habits that annoyed, amused and upset me. No doubt some of the traits of my generation annoyed, amused and upset them. Some of their reasoning was inexplicable.

"You don't do that," was the famous line, always said in a surprised tone and often accompanied by the equally famous, "Everybody knows that..." in a confident, you-should-know-better tone.

For instance, if we were out together and I needed a drink, I might buy a pint of cold milk and, to my great satisfaction and physical relief, drink it all down there and then. All eyes turned to me.

"You don't do that! Everyone knows that you take milk home, pour a cup, then sit down and drink it!"

Or a variation:

"You don't drink milk like that, you take it home and warm up a cupful. Hot milk is what you drink, no one drinks cold milk, especially a whole pint AND out of the bottle. Strange you are, people will be talking about you!"

It was the same if I drank a bottle of soda pop when we were out.

"You don't do that, you take pop home and share it."

"I asked if anyone wanted some, I offered to buy it."

"Not the point. You do not drink a bottle of pop like that, you take it home!"

"But home is hours away and we are very thirsty now!"

"That is not the point, we will have a cup of something when we find a café."

"But this shop right here sells pop, juice and milk, big bottles, small bottles, room temperature and cold ones."

"That is not the point."

Early one Good Friday Terry knocked at my door. We are going to walk up Twmbarlwm, he told me. A long-standing tradition, he said, confident as always.

"Everyone does it on Good Friday."

First I had heard of it, but why not? I put on my shoes and coat and headed for the bus stop.

"We walk," said Terry.

"Walk! Duw, there's Twmbarlwm," I said, pointing; it was visible from our front garden. Not only was it the other side of Newport, it was a long way outside of Newport.

"A bloody long walk that. You're not kidding me?"

"No, shut up, you are doing bugger all else. Come on."

Terry was insistent.

"We can go on our bikes?"

"No."

We walked into town, easy enough; we walked out the

other side, easy enough. Approaching Ridgeway we saw other groups determinedly plodding in the same direction. Terry was right. The closer we got to Twmbarlwm the slower our pace became, for the lane was choked with people, hundreds of them, all steadfastly plodding to Twmbarlwm, then scrambling up to the pimple. It took four hours there, four hours back, and not an open shop anywhere. On aching feet I trudged wearily onwards. Not a bite to eat, not a drop to drink, until we arrived back at our side of Newport and found a shop open. We each bought a frozen Jubbly and frenziedly gnawed and sucked as we hobbled home.

A view around Newport towards Twmbarlwm
(courtesy of Paul Flynn, MP)

It is thought that this tradition, which continues to this day, goes back to medieval times, when Twmbarlwm was on the route of the Cistercian pilgrimage trail. This was the last time that I walked to Twmbarlwm and the last time that I walked anywhere with Terry.

By 1961, Llanwern Steelworks was well into construction. We were young teenage boys, adventurous and curious.

On a sunny weekend day we went into the works and cycled openly along the road, looking here, asking there. The workmen were friendly, answering our questions, chatting – until the day a security Land Rover deliberately drove into us and we were hauled dazed, confused and bruised, carrying damaged bikes, into the security centre and given a hard time. We were reported to the police and our school. Why did they not just stop us and say, "Hey, lads, it's dangerous here and you are a nuisance; get out..." Authority was arrogant.

In October 1962 the Queen opened Llanwern Steelworks, known as Spencer Works as the first general manager was a Mr Spencer. We were given the day off school to line the route and play at being grateful peasants. We turned up – it was something different to do, we were fifteen and there were girls. We had not the slightest interest in, nor respect for, royalty. We booed when they drove by. Teenage bravado, or did we mean it? What had they ever done for us? Our teachers and parents were royalists, but they were unable to explain why. We asked them why and they stuttered a few banalities. All they really said was, "because".

It was about this time, after a Sunday communion, that I walked over the transporter bridge with fellow churchgoers and young teens Robin Thomas, Larry Sutherland and David Bourne. I do not know who suggested it; it was not me. I went along because I was too scared to say no and did not want the gang to know that I was scared. All the way I was hoping the others would talk themselves out of it. In our Sunday suits we left church, and sauntered along the black ash path to Corporation Road and on to the bridge. All the way

I acted nonchalant, while my stomach churned. We waited for the transporter to come across, unload and load the cars and the operator to take our sixpences and open the gate for us. We climbed and climbed and climbed. At the top, exhibiting a nonchalance that we did not have, we strolled across, over the dirty grey Usk, with its steep banks of evil-looking, black, gluttonous, alluvial mud. Down the other side we waited for the operator to let us out and rode the transporter back across to our own side and strode briskly home for Sunday lunch. I went up the bridge twice more after that, again because I was too scared to say no.

Most Sundays I walked to my grandparents for Sunday lunch. Gran always cooked succulent roast beef, boiled potatoes and a gravy to die for. As a treat we sometimes had a Kunzle cake after lunch. Occasionally Gran also made the most marvellous fruit cake. She never ate her meals with Granddad and myself. My father said that she had never eaten at the same table as men. I never knew why.

I had started attending church when I was twelve, for communion. My parents were religious, going to church every week, sometimes twice. They were involved in church fêtes, Mothers' Union and generally helping out when needed. It was expected that I be confirmed. I was too young to argue and had been brainwashed by the system. Like most people then, I had faith and belief, and I was terrified of hell's fire. I went to my first communion class because of strong psychological family pressure. I continued to go for the same reason and because it was *something* different to do. It was, in fact, something to do. There were people of my own age and, more importantly, girls. I had just started to notice girls. I had my first shave before going to one of these communion classes. I removed the light brown, soft haired growth on my upper lip. I started shaving regularly at twelve or thirteen. After being confirmed I attended church regularly.

When in a pique though, I said such things as, "How do you know there is a God?" and "The Bible does not make sense!" Adults immediately turned to me, their faces angry, flushed, scared.

"How dare you say that!", "You will go to hell, you will", "Wash your mouth out," they snapped, glaring at me.

"Oh, David, don't talk like that," Gran wailed.

They were in a panic, maybe for my soul, maybe for what others might think of them. Unquestioning belief in an unprovable concept was demanded, centuries of brainwashing showing in their alarm.

At fourteen, I spent Friday evenings at the Church Youth Club with Lyndon, Terry, the brothers Ian and Keith James, and our girlfriends. Mine at the time was Marilyn, who was fourteen, with a sexy sylph-like figure, light blonde hair and blue eyes. Keith was one of those irritating sods who's extremely handsome, charming, has a way with words and is liked by girls, mothers and grandmothers. He always had a beauty in tow; the other youths struggled, though Terry less so.

The new vicar, Vicar Davies, from the more disciplined valleys, set up a Friday evening youth club and tried hard to arrange interesting events for us. We were youths; we did not want organised things. He complained about my kissing Marilyn – it was tongue in mouth stuff, hand under blouse. We were of the opinion that this was what teenagers had always done; where was the problem here? But Marilyn's mother had seen the bites on her neck – any more of them and she threatened to march Marilyn around to my place to show my mother. This would have been bad, for Mam and Dad would have felt duty bound to nag me for ages. I stopped biting Marilyn's neck and tried groping instead. Marilyn was having none of that.

It was expected that youngsters did as they were told, and follow the directives of the establishment. Most youngsters obeyed, as their parents had and their parents before them. This was discipline; it taught one to conform, it made one a useful, albeit cowed, member of society. What will happen when my generation has gone and a more aware generation moves up? Then the populace will have no superstitious dread and the Church no control over the population.

At fifteen I decided that the Church was not for me. I cannot exactly say why I gave up on it. I feel a lot of things came together at that time. I read a lot, I thought a lot, I questioned. The Church did not gel, it did not feel right. There were too many unanswerable questions; there was too much living in the past, too much expecting blind faith. Far too much arrogance, far too much establishment. We were told that poverty is fundamental to Christianity. Yet we read that the Church of England was mega rich, the biggest landowner in the kingdom, with many fine buildings and large investments. The robes of the archbishops were said to cost thousands of pounds. But whenever our parish church needed something, the ordinary people were browbeaten to come up with the money. It was the church of the state, not the church of the people, not the church of the Bible. With cracks appearing in our society, where was the binding force? Since time immemorial a belief system of some sort has held communities together, guided them, led them, coerced them, in good times and bad. Where was it then, when it was needed? Where was the strong, ultimate force? Where were the fire and brimstone zealots to draw a line in the sand and say, "Thou shalt not cross"?

The Church, the representation of the most powerful, no longer led. It was lost. I noted the duplicity of it, too. The worst possible disaster and it is, "Praise the Lord" as we bury dead children. Win a victory, or a fortune, and again, "Praise the Lord". Heads I win, tails I win. I did not accept this. I think back to the brainwashing of my childhood, all about sin and the punishment of sinners and I think, *What a load of nonsense*. To mock the indoctrination I scribbled the following verses:

One day we shall pay for our sins,
those made in haste and at leisure,
what we mete out returns to bite,
reckoning comes at its pleasure.

Unintended sins have no cost,
for these we are seen not to blame,
rather those who proclaim it sin,
must explain why they seek our shame.

Naive sins we make by mistake,
for these the cost we pay is low,
of these each of us is guilty,
for these are wrongs we did not know.

Minor sins as made by us all,
out of error, anger or heat,
carry a small cost to be paid,
retribution we cannot cheat.

Venial sins carry a cost,
measured according to their worth,
these have an ultimate total,
tallied against people from birth.

Mortal sins are as commanded,
all ten must be well known by all,
but there are more hurtful actions,
alongside which other acts pall.

Deeds ill meant are never forgot,
they merely wait and bide their time,
the payment extracted is great,
no one is forgiven this crime.

Indolent now our faces turned,
does God resent his being spurned?
now from wherever God may be,
do angels sigh for you and me?

10. Teenage Angst

At fourteen I had gone through a growth spurt and started exercising. This had given me a better physique, although I was still podgy and bad at gymnastics and games. I decided I needed to change.

At fifteen I went to the YMCA and asked to join the weight-lifting club. Charming, kind, sensitive Mr Bakewell took me up the rickety wooden stairs to the attic and there it was and there were they. It was plain that a newcomer was not wanted, especially one so young, podgy and of a gentle disposition. These were roughs. I was later to learn that some of them were known to the police; very well known. Others, who were not known, should have been. The rest were honest, straightforward brutes. I had not come so far to chicken out. I joined in and was ignored. After a few weeks they began helping me. After a few months I was one of them.

During this period I was walking five kilometres to school and the same back, five days a week. I was walking a three-kilometre paper route six mornings a week and six evenings, plus the Sunday morning route with two heavy sacks which I went back and refilled halfway around. Three evenings a week I walked five kilometres to the YMCA for a heavy, two-hour workout and walked back home. On Friday evenings, after working out, we went to the local swimming bath and swam lengths. On Saturdays I often ran a few kilometres. I was a fit young teenager. Later in my teens, close to full height – just under one-point-eight metres – I weighed eighty kilograms and was able to lift more than my body weight above my head, bench-press a hundred kilograms with ease and lift one hundred and sixty kilograms up to my hips. How I long for those days as I puff to do up my trousers.

Age 16, at the beach

By my mid-teens times had changed: my father was earning more money, we bought a washing machine and a refrigerator, and I was given five shillings a week pocket money, which was a lot in those days. Granddad also gave me a shilling a week. I had the paper round, which paid thirty shillings a week. I raked in thirty-six shillings a week. In today's money this is one pound and eighty pence, but then three pints of lager, a beef curry with rice, chapattis, poppadoms and pickle, followed by ice cream, cost me thirteen shillings, or sixty-five pence in decimal money.

I bought my first beer when I was fourteen; publicans did not ask for proof of age then. I had cycled to Nash one summer evening with the boys. We were all thirsty, so out of bravado I walked into the Waterloo and bought a half pint of Skol lager, with a dash of lime juice, for one shilling and four pence. I took it outside and drank it in front of the gang. They were impressed. I felt Mr Big. They asked that I buy for them, but I did not, for us big boys had to be responsible for the youngsters.

By this stage I had two vices. One was a few pints on a Friday evening with the reprobates from the YMCA weight-lifting club. I especially remember Tony (Ant) Edwards, an infrequent member. He lived with his parents in our avenue, across the road and five doors along. One Friday evening Ant and I swam in the Usk at Caerleon. I was sick for days, for the Usk is a dirty river. In 1974 Ant was jailed for the attempted murder of his father-in-law, after attacking him with a shotgun. At the turn of the century he was still inside. Somehow, it does not seem right, considering it was a family fight with wrong on both sides.

My other vice was mauling Josie on Saturdays. She was a cute little dumpling, with plenty of the right things in the right places. I never fancied her, but she was obliging. I had a crush on Liz, one of our gang and an extremely attractive girl: intelligent, well mannered, with a beautiful face and a trim, shapely figure. I delivered papers to her house, but did not have the confidence to approach her. In 2000 I learned that she had died of cancer in 1985, in her mid-thirties. I had last seen her in 1968, but in 2000 I felt sad.

I had panic attacks when I heard my parents whispering, for it was usually about me. Following a bout of whispering one sunny evening in summer, my parents appeared in my room.

"David, we want to talk to you."

What now? Did someone see me boozing, did Josie mouth to her parents, who did I last slap and when? My brothers had just, somehow, disappeared, again. My parents never drank, smoked, swore or fooled around. My three brothers and I were surely a disappointment.

"We found a ten shilling note in the back pocket of your trousers." Mam goes through the pockets before putting stuff in the washing machine.

"Ah," I said with relief, "thanks."

"We are not angry." Pause. "Say where you got it and we will say no more." Both heads nodding.

"Eh?" Were they joking? "It's mine!"

"It's a lot of money, David. Where did you get it?" Mam wheedled.

"Hey, come on now, I get thirty-six shillings a week, *you know that!*"

"That is not enough to *miss* ten shillings. Don't lie, we know you stole it. Don't talk to us like that. *Now*, where did you get it?"

After much arguing the ten shillings was begrudgingly returned to me.

Mam ironed everything: socks, underpants, towels, pullovers, pyjamas, the lot. Shirts and trousers I appreciated, but underpants! Who wants sharp creases in them? Mam also washed every utensil after use. Fill a cup with fresh tap water to top up a simmering saucepan and she washed the cup, with the same tap water. I sometimes hoped that I was adopted.

The affair of the black shirt was disturbing. I had seen either a movie or a television programme in which the hero had worn a black shirt. It made him look cool, suave, debonair and handsome. I wanted to look cool, suave, debonair and handsome. I wanted a black shirt.

"Mam, will you buy me a black shirt?" I asked in all innocence.

God, that opened the door to a non-stop tirade.

"Why do you want a black shirt? When are you going to wear it? You have joined the Nazi party, haven't you, haven't you? You will get into trouble, you will be arrested. Why do you want a black shirt?" my mother started.

When Dad arrived home he got it before the door had closed after him.

"David wants a black shirt. Tell him Bill, tell him he will get into trouble, that he will be arrested. Tell him how naughty he is and what will happen," Mam continued.

"You are not having a black shirt. You are not joining the Nazis. It took us years and a lot of men to stop them! You are not joining them! You will get into trouble with the police. Why do you want a black shirt?" Dad had joined the misdirected rant.

Granddad arrived later and he was immediately indoctrinated.

"You cannot have a black shirt, David. You will get into trouble. Why do you want a black shirt? Have you joined the Mosley party? Are you a Nazi?" he sang from the same sheet.

Every time I tried to explain, I was drowned out by repetitions of their arguments and cries of "liar!" Gran was told too: when I visited her, tears rolled down her cheeks as she pleaded with me not to wear a black shirt. Even Uncle Harry and Aunty Beat had a go at me.

This was the first I knew of black shirts being associated with Nazis and Sir Oswald Mosley. Until then, I had thought that Nazis mostly wore brown or green shirts as shown in the movies. Until then I had not heard of Mosley. I only wanted a shirt.

When I was a toddler I had thrown temper tantrums. If I did not get my own way, or thought myself to have been unfairly judged, I cried, stamped and made a nuisance of myself. I was often a great embarrassment to my parents. Later, as a child, I had moped and sulked if I did not get my own way, or thought myself insulted. As a young teenager I wept with rage when thwarted, or perceived myself to have been wronged. I lay awake at night, tears in my eyes, wondering how to avenge myself. Luckily I outgrew this trait by the time I reached my late teens, for by then I was a strong, fit fellow; more than capable of seriously hurting anyone I chose to attack. In my early teens I started writing poetry. The first one that I kept was about my suppressed anger and thoughts of vengeance.

Tired, but I cannot go to sleep,
for a bitter rage that makes me weep
and dark thoughts of vengeance I will take,
of lashing out for their bones to break.

Of eyes I will gouge and throats squeeze
and nothing shall my wrath appease,
I imagine my fists, head and feet,
brutally striking in anger's heat.

I think of spite that wants me broken,
and threats implied but never spoken,
their one-sided tale holds all in thrall,
my story not listened to at all.

I shall take the chance for which I ache,
to play a game that they cannot fake,
making my fists and hands red and raw,
gleefully having evened the score.

I will give no heed to cries or pleas,
but will smash the bastards to their knees,
I shall revel in their running gore,
smashing until I can smash no more.

I want to hurt them for all their lies,
to see stark awareness in their eyes,
as I hit and hit and feel their pain,
then do the same again and again.

I know violence is not the way,
futile, it shall not my rage allay,
best one day under an open sky,
approach and quietly ask them "Why?"

I had actually started out writing risqué limericks to amuse my friends, and this in turn, led to poems. Whilst I placed my limericks anonymously on doors around the school, I kept quiet about the poetry, for it was considered sissy stuff. Not exactly Keats, but the poems amused me.

Old man Prichard, tall and slim, and his wife, short and dumpy, owned and operated the little newsagent where I worked. His name was said to be Ebenezer, and she was addressed as Florrie. Ebb and Flow we called them. Did you know, the Welsh once had the equivalent of 'Mac'? It was 'Ap' meaning 'son of'. If its use had not died out following the Acts of Union in 1536, I would be David Ap Hughes. In protest many dropped the 'A', capitalised the 'p' and put it in front of their family names. Mr Ap Richard became Mr Prichard and Ap Owen became Bowen, the 'p' hardened to a 'b'. Have a look at Welsh family names starting with 'P' or 'B'. Take off the 'P' or 'B' and in many cases you are still left with a name.

I carried an air pistol in my paper bag; it was legal then. When a dog came for me during my paper round, I let it get on my ankle, then shot through a hole in the bag. The dog yelped like crazy and ran around in circles. The owners inevitably ran out.

"What did you do?"

My reaction was to shrug, look pityingly at the frenzied wretch and say, "Nothing – must be distemper.

He just bit my ankle then went crazy."

"He did not bite your ankle." Forced denial with a hint of panic. Ah! They knew he was a biter.

"Yes he did... ask them," I said pointing to someone.

If the neighbour had seen the incident, then they agreed. If they had not, then there was a chance they would agree if the dog was a known biter. The owner shut up. Sometimes, the wound bled and the pellet had to be cut out. Next time I was delivering papers there, out they stormed.

"You shot our dog!" they said, as loud as was possible without shouting.

"After he bit me," said I.

Again, "You shot our dog!"

"Just you wait there; my husband will be out now," the women usually said.

I waited. If they came out and saw I was hefty and ready to fight, they apologised for the dog having bitten me. I had to shoot some of those dogs two or three times before they learnt their lesson.

We were legally armed in those days. I had an air rifle, an air pistol, a bow, pocket knives of many shapes and sizes, and sheath knives with 150 mm blades – all legally purchased over the counter of sports shops. Roger Baser had a paper round at the same newsagent. I went with him to buy his first pistol. He paid nine pounds nine shillings for a Webley Senior, 0.22 calibre. We went to the nearest post office and bought a licence for seven shillings and six pence. That was a powerful pistol. I was saving up to buy a Webley .22 rifle with telescopic sights; the ultimate in youthful firepower. For cats and dogs it was the Orphan Maker.

Another weapon we had was the potato gun, also called a spud gun. This had long been a child's toy and could be purchased from any toyshop. New, improved, more robust models were always coming out. When I was about fifteen, the latest was a solid little beauty, about the size of a Derringer. It had a shell case identical to that of a revolver. A cap, for an ordinary cap gun, was put in the case. The case was then pushed into a potato and a piece broken off. This was loaded into the gun and fired. At a range of two metres it stung if it hit exposed skin. Ever innovative, we obtained handfuls of shell cases and pre-made potato pieces that we let dry, and bought shotgun powder from the sports shop. We pressed a few caps into the case, added a sprinkle of powder, forced hard potato on top of these, oiled our gun barrels and we were ready. Those things hurt. At break time the schoolyard sounded to the bang, bang, bang of numerous guns and the wailing of the wounded. Whole gangs hunted down victims; some boys had two or three guns. If you were cornered you had it, unless your own gang shot a way out for you. Usually they were watching from out of range, cheering on the shooters. In the space of a few seconds you expected at least a dozen hits on the legs and neck, from point-blank range. The masters let us get on with it; I think they were pleased to see us playing macho games.

The masters also ignored our game of stretch. Two boys stood face to face, a metre apart. In turns we threw knives into the ground. Where the knife landed, the boy who was on the receiving end had to put his foot against it. The idea was to stretch one's opponent's legs apart, until he could no longer stand. Injuries were many, but slight; to make a show of it was considered sissy.

At fifteen I rang a doorbell and ran away for the last time. It was in the street where I delivered papers, the estate where I had once collected empty pop bottles. The house of choice was two down from the corner shop. It had no fence, no gate, an extremely short path and a big, glowing bell of the wonderful ding-dong-ding-dong chime. I was in and out before I knew it.

My companion that night was short Leslie and he was already past the shop and haring over Nash Road, his little legs a blur. I trotted along after him. I heard and felt the door open and someone come out. I hoped I was far enough away not to be recognised. I heard someone come after me. I knew he was a fit man from the beat of his footsteps. I thought to have the no-hoper after me for fifty metres or so. I moved up from trot to steady lope. After the psychological fifty metres, he was still with me and coming on well. I decided to finish him quickly; I had things do to. I had a very fast pace for a mile. Not many teenagers were able to run a mile, never mind at my pace. I was going to burn him off.

I headed for the long road. I was better on the straight – cornering at speed I never mastered. I put my foot down and went. I took him the full mile. But he stayed with me. Now I was apprehensive. I could easily run miles at a good jog but could not hold this fast pace for more than a mile. I went down to a jog, but after five minutes he was still with me, and gaining. He had invested a lot of time and effort in this and was going to see it through. I guessed he was very angry; he was obviously fit. I settled into my jog, hoping to keep the lead long enough to discourage him. Maybe his supper was getting cold, or he was missing his favourite television programme and he would turn back. I stopped, turned and waited. If it came to a fight I did not want him getting me from behind, nor did I want to be winded. Nor did I want to be far from anywhere. I had a fence on one side, a wide reen on the other; not the best position for flight or fight, where flight was out of the question. He came on, slowing to a fast walk; he was roughly my height, but not as well built. He stopped twenty metres away to regain his breath.

Uh-oh, thought I.

From his position he shouted, "Did you just ring my doorbell?"

What a dumb question; of course I had, he had seen me legging it.

"Yes," I shouted back.

"Why?"

I dread that question. I can never answer it. I threw in a distraction.

"How did you manage to keep up?"

"I'm a professional football player. Don't do it again," said he and walked away.

By the time I got to Josie's it was late; she had gone out.

An event I remember well was Boxing Day evening 1962. I was in Terry's house, with Ian and his brother Keith. There were a few girls there; Terry was a master at organising such things. It was a well-behaved affair, for Terry's parents were present. We left late evening. Keith was first out of the front door and called us to look. There was something about his call, so we crowded to see.

"Snow!"

"Wow, we have snow."

"Where did that come from?" We had not felt cold in the house.

The winter of 1962-3 was the coldest in England and Wales since 1740. A belt of rain over northern Scotland on 24 December turned to snow as it moved south. The snow belt reached southern England on Boxing Day and stopped. Anticyclones from the east brought bitterly cold winds day after day. Depressions brought snow. A blizzard over South Wales on 29 and 30 December brought snowdrifts several metres deep. Mean maximum temperatures for January 1963 were more than five degrees Celsius below average over most of Wales, and much the same in February. Villages were cut off, roads and railways were blocked, telephone wires were brought down, things ground to a crawl, coal stocks froze; the school had no coal so we were sent home.

It was a great time for a fifteen-year-old. From a safe distance, with an escape route behind us, we pelted all and sundry with snowballs. The most exciting was to ambush the Nash bus at the roundabout next to Spytty Park. The road was so badly and deeply rutted with compacted snow that only buses travelled it, and these traversed the ruts in first gear, creeping along at walking speed. At the Spytty roundabout they had to stop.

We positioned ourselves in Spytty Park. Between us and the bus was a waist-high fence, a two-metre wide reen with two-metre high banks, and finally a pavement covered with a metre of snow – an impregnable position against even the most suicidal and frustrated of bus crews. Here we waited, giggling, snowballs at the ready. The bus slowed and crawled past our position to stop at the roundabout. The driver did not want to; the conductor definitely did not want to. In the 1960s, Newport buses did not have doors. The entrance at the rear left-hand side – our target – was permanently open. In a moment of stupidity the conductor might be standing there, or so we hoped. From the moment the bus started to slow down until it had crawled out of range, barrage after barrage of snowballs, pitched with unerring accuracy, pounded through the entrance. Once out of range, the conductor gave us our reward and encouragement: the poor sod let loose and swore at us.

Ian, my long-term buddy and confidant, was considered by most to be a bad boy. He was no naughtier than any of us though; he was just caught more often. He was of average height and build, intelligent, and ready for anything if there was profit, or a laugh.

The Easter after the bad winter we went camping in the Brecon Beacons. I had my small tent and we both had ordinary sleeping bags, but we survived and enjoyed ourselves. The first day, Dad drove us to the mountains. We did not know where we were going; we just said, "stop," when we saw a likely place, climbed out and marched off in high spirits.

The first night we pitched camp alongside a forestry reserve, where a pile of post poles was stacked on the track. It was cold, so we took a few fence poles for our fire. They had been treated with creosote, and so they burned – did they burn! With a frying pan held at arm's length we charcoaled a few sausages and ate the best bits.

That first night under canvas was what it was all about. We were going to take turns on UFO watch, but ten minutes of listening to the night passed, then all of a sudden it was morning. Breakfast was better: we used small bits of wood for a fire. We had three days of adventure, walking, talking, looking, listening, camping near streams, as we followed our map on a trail towards home.

Putting the tent up and taking it down again was a bind, but it was too cold and wet to sleep without a tent. We had no wet weather clothes, only sweaters and a donkey jacket each, but they were more than enough.

By the fourth day we were lost in thick mist, way up a mountain. We stopped and waited, but the mist persisted. We were in no danger; we had the tent, sleeping bags, warm clothes, food and water. We decided to move slowly. Tying ourselves together with a rope, four metres apart, we moved across the mountain until we came to a stream. This we followed down to where it met another stream and became bigger. In thick mist we followed, not without some difficulty and detour, until we were following a respectable waterway. When it brought us to a well-used track we parted company with the water and headed down. Soon we were on a small, tarred lane. The mist had lifted but we were lost. There was a suitable camping spot across a stream, so we forded the stream and set up camp for the night. We thought we might go home the next day. We dried our socks and boots near the fire. My boots were too near and they split, rendering them useless, so now we had to get off the mountain quickly. I had tennis shoes in my bag so I put these on and slept in them. The next day we crossed the stream again and walked, our wet footwear drying on our feet. We flagged down a van coming from behind us.

"Hi, boys, I'm going to Birmingham, where you going?"

"Newport."

"Out of my way that is, but drop you convenient I can, see."

"Okay, thanks."

"Get in the back, boys."

It was a laundry van. The back was full of dirty clothes in white sacks and we made ourselves comfortable. After many miles the van stopped and the driver banged on the partition.

"Here you are, boys. Cross the road, stand on the corner, soon get a lift to Newport, you will," he shouted to us.

We looked at each other. I had a thought and itchy feet; an instant decision was made.

"Can you take us to Birmingham?"

"No problem."

Nana Knight lived in the Midlands. I did not need boots there, so why go home so soon? Ian and I had a few days in Arley before hitch-hiking home.

During the summer holiday of 1963 we cycled the one hundred and sixty kilometres to Weymouth. Ian had it all worked out. He bought an army surplus bell tent for three pounds ten shillings. He toured scrapyards for timber, bicycle wheels and all sorts. He made a very respectable cart and attachment for his bicycle. It looked rough, but it was sturdy and efficient. With a little practice we were able to pack everything neatly in the cart. We were to take turns riding the bike with the cart attached.

We left one Friday evening from Ian's house, cycling

down Nash Road past our paper shop. Ebb and Flow were standing outside their shop with all the paperboys, my parents, customers, our friends. We were cheered and waved on our way. Waving most enthusiastically was Keith. He was glad to see us gone for two weeks. He was to do both our paper rounds and be locum for other boys who were off on summer holiday. With luck, he would make over four pounds in the two weeks.

We cycled the country lanes to Severn Tunnel Junction and took a train under the Severn to Bristol. We cycled through Bristol and took the road south. At two in the morning we stopped in a field, ate our sandwiches, lay on our backs and fell asleep under the stars. We were on the road early in the morning, stopping at a bus station for sandwiches. A kilometre farther on I took the fast bike and went back for more sandwiches. I did not see Ian again for three days. He had taken one road, I searched up and down another. I went on to Weymouth and sent a postcard to his home address.

"Having a nice time, wish you were here," it read.

Ian had dumped the cart with a kind household and cycled home with the news that I was lost. My being lost did not upset Ian, but having his adventure ruined did annoy him. My parents reported me as a missing person. A policeman came to the house for a description; my Uncle Jim told the policeman I had a big mouth.

I slept the first night in a barn and had breakfast in a truckers' café. The next night I slept in a field; I did not have enough money for bed and breakfast accommodation.

The third day, late afternoon, I was walking through the crowds on the Weymouth seafront, wondering where to sleep that night, when I heard a shout:

"Hughes, you arsehole!"

It was Ian. He was in the passenger seat of his father's car; his dad had brought him to Weymouth. I was relieved. Ian had already set up the tent in a good camping ground; he had collected the tent on his way back to Weymouth. He intended to have his camping holiday with or without me. He had pitched the tent on a hard piece of drained ground and hammered home our home-made, extra long, extra strong tent pegs.

We cycled around the Weymouth area, swam in the sea, lay on the beach, cooked on a gas stove outside our tent and did not wash all the while we were there. Our old army bell tent did not fit in with all the other smart, colourful, purpose-made tents and we were two, young, scruffy peasants. We were pariahs in the bottom corner of the big field. One weekend Ian's parents came to visit – four of us in the tent and room to spare. Another weekend my parents and my brothers came to visit – seven of us in the tent and still room to spare, although not much. We managed to push my brother Geoffrey into the fire. A pan of boiling water scalded his arm, and he was rushed to hospital. He recovered in a few days.

While my parents were staying with us, a fierce storm swept the campsite. We did know about it until we scrambled out of our sturdy, well-anchored tent in the morning. There was a scene of devastation: tent fabric was wrapped around trees and electricity pylons, and colourful tents floated in the sea, littered the beach and draped themselves over hedges and cars. We cooked and ate breakfast as the other campers salvaged what they could.

Our main objective was to pick up girls. We tried, but

we were inexperienced, unsophisticated, gauche and pretty smelly. A shame, as ours was a spacious tent.

Our two-week holiday was over. The trip back was uneventful; we cycled from Weymouth to Bristol non-stop, missed the last train to Severn Tunnel Junction and slept on the station that night, on a plank in a flooded storeroom, our bikes and cart in with us. We took the early morning train, arriving at Severn Tunnel Junction, exhausted, ravenous and dirty, not long after the sun rose. We cycled through the country lanes with happy hearts and were finally on Nash Road. As we approached the houses, near Lliswerry, there was Lyndon sitting on the wall of his parents' house, waiting for us with a smirk on his face. He had figured out when we would arrive and got up early for the occasion. We gabbled the story of our adventure and followed him into his house, hoping Aunty Glad would give us food. No chance; Aunty Glad was not having that. Uncle Tom was equally unsympathetic; he called us "silly young buggers".

I miss the summer days of my youth. In the afternoons we played games at school. In the evenings we played mixed tennis in Beechwood Park. On Saturdays and Sundays we fished on the common, cycled around the countryside, climbed hills and trees, picnicked in woods and walked through town window-shopping. At weekends we were out all day, until hunger drove us home in the evening. There was no frozen food then, no ready meals. All our food was fresh and natural and cooked then and there – meat, two veg, gravy, bread, and enough of it. No arguing, no preferences, no claims of 'allergies' – we ate what was put in front of us. Our mothers could not cook to save their lives, but we were hungry, so we ate.

It was not until the 1960s, when foreigners came to Newport, that we knew what food could taste like. Not only were their curry and chop suey different and tasty, but they produced something completely different in taste, texture and appearance. They did not rinse the life out of food, they did not drown it in water and they did not overcook it. Our parents knew no better. All fruit, vegetable and meat were well rinsed. Vegetables, especially cabbage and greens, were boiled for hours in a lot of water. Mince meat was put in a colander and held under the hot tap, the wash water running red from the colander then becoming paler. The mince was put in a pan, liberally covered with water and bought to the boil early afternoon.

"There, that will be ready when Dad comes home tonight," Mam would declare.

The house smelled of the food from midday, when cooking started, to evening, when we ate the insipid slurry. I asked why we had to rinse everything under the tap.

"To get off the germs, of course," was the learned reply.

"But that only does the surface," I continued. "Most are inside the food. Cooking it in boiling water, or a hot oven, will kill everything."

No, it had to be rinsed. Our food was awash in weak, watery gravy and served with no thought for presentation, in a room that stank of its cooking. Our parents did not prepare food, they fought it.

Later, in my first year of university, a girlfriend made me a cottage pie in less than thirty minutes from start to finish. She put Oxo, herbs and carrots into the mince, salt in the potatoes; little fuss, no rinsing. It tasted marvellous. Like a missionary going among the heathen I took my secrets back to Wales. These new-fangled ways took time to catch on, and when I went back to England my parents slid back into their old ways. I had sympathy for Moses.

On Saturday evenings the boys in the gang went to the last show at the cinema. We bought our tickets in twos, pretending we did not know anyone else. They did not like letting gangs in – gangs were rowdy, we were rowdy. In those days most cinemas had a downstairs and an upstairs. The upstairs was called the balcony, sometimes the circle; it cost a few pence more than downstairs. We sat upstairs at the front. We participated with orchestrated, "Look out behind you" and loud, drawn-out "Oooo"s. We had fun, even if we were thrown out. Lyndon's giggling and loud guffaws were the deciding factor. The show stopped, lights came on and all the male ushers appeared. We knew a policeman was lurking outside.

"All right you lot, out, the lot of you."

"Us?"

"Why?" a chorus.

"You bloody well know why. Out!" Lyndon by now giving out full belly laughs.

"It wasn't us, honest." Our giggling giving the lie to this.

Straight faced, looking serious and hard done by, we all pointed at the nearest, harmless-looking people.

"It was them, honest," we said.

Three old ladies looked panic-stricken.

"We will help you throw them out."

"Bloody well out, now, you buggers."

"Oooo, language!" we harmonised, except Lyndon who was now on his knees, spluttering and wiping his eyes.

"We want our money back," we argued down the stairs.

Outside Lyndon fought for self-control, the policeman smiled and we left. A good night out.

Sometimes, in a moment of weakness, or outright stupidity a parent allowed their child to have a party at home. I never did; I knew what people like me were capable of. Usually it was the girls who had a birthday party and told their friends to bring some boys along.

Come the night of the party, a Friday or Saturday, there we were, sixteen years old, clean and neat, with a present for the birthday girl. We also brought booze to the house and hid it in the front garden. Mummies, grannies and aunties looked at us patronisingly, simpering, telling each other what handsome, well set-up boys we were.

"And only sixteen too! Never think to look at them," they cooed.

After an hour the ice was broken, kids were dancing, the buffet had taken punishment, guests were in and out, the adults had retreated to another room and Sods Incorporated brought in the booze. Then it was heavy petting all over the house. We were considerate: we collected the empty bottles and put them in a neighbour's garden. Birthday girl chose the neighbour. The house was left a shambles, birthday girl and her mates had been well and truly groped and no doubt a lot were sick that night. Birthday girl had status; once her mates had recovered they agreed it was a great party, and we were invited to others. We never disappointed and were never caught out. Goodness knows how the birthday girl's parents reacted.

We had parties at Lyndon's house too, when his parents were away, though no one was silly enough to damage anything. Booze was plentiful. We organised it in advance, all chipping in to help. Lyndon bought simple foodstuff: bread, cheese, corned beef. These were on the kitchen table and we made sandwiches as the riot progressed. Beer was in the refrigerator, wine on the kitchen draining board. For hard liquor, ask Lyndon and he gave you some from upstairs. We all arrived with bottles as well.

Lyndon's house was on the outskirts of town, just in the country, in a short row of semis. It was quiet and the neighbours were no problem. We kicked off at seven, ran low on booze by nine and were shaken down by Lyndon for more money – girls and boys. He took all the cash we had – and we had plenty – then threw in a lot of his own and gave it to Dougie, who had a car, to go to the off-licence for cheap beer. Dougie returned and off we went again. The inside loo was for the girls; boys peed behind the garage. The back of the garden was for throwing up – girls and boys. By the time we left it was past midnight; there were no sleepovers then.Fourteen-to eighteen-year-olds staggered along the street at one in the morning, peeing every hundred yards, throwing up every now and again, girls crying, boys swearing, all singing. Then trying to get your key in the lock and sneak into bed. Next morning whispering to your folks that you must have eaten a bad pork pie at the church youth club social last night and you will stay in your room for a while.

Late one morning, Mr and Mrs Hill arrived. I heard Mrs Hill talking loudly to Mam at the front door.

"I am not saying it was your David, but he was there," she was saying. "You should have seen the state our Petulia came home in this morning. Come here Petulia, come here and let Mrs Hughes see."

I carefully peered out of my window. Mr Hill was still behind the wheel, staring straight ahead. The beautiful, fourteen-year-old Petulia was sprawled across the back seat. She made a valiant effort to get out, threw up, swore and crumpled sobbing on the pavement. I retreated to my bed.

On warm summer evenings we hung out in Spytty Park, the boys grouping together, the girls gathered only a few metres away. For some reason we did not date girls in our gang; well, not seriously. It was a good feeling just to be there, with friends. We hung around talking until someone suggested something of interest, then we acted on it. Leaving the girls, we jumped on our bikes to go scrumping, or to the sea wall, or to ride through the lanes.

On Bonfire Night we were at our naughtiest. A pocket full of penny-bangers, a lighter and we were off to annoy. Bangers cost a penny each, hence the name. We bought twelve for a shilling in any shop in town, yet we let Lyndon talk us into buying from him. Lyndon could get boxes of bangers, each containing a gross. The total cost was twelve shillings; more money than we wanted to spend, for more bangers than we needed, but Lyndon had his way. On Bonfire Night every boy and girl in the gang had a gross of bangers and a lighter. With surplus ammunition and so many of us, we must have been a real nuisance as we threw bangers into all the gardens. Of course, we thought it was great fun.

At sixteen I wanted a motorbike. I bought a BSA, model C11G, a single cylinder 250 cc. It cost me ten pounds. I bought a fairing, crash bars, helmet and goggles for a lot more – leaving little money for petrol. It was a bit of a lemon and it did not help that I kept falling off. I rode it to school to cut a dash. A few of us at school, all in the thickos' class, had motorbikes and we had to keep them outside the gate. It took all my money. I lost interest in it after six months and sold it.

I had no steady girlfriend at this stage; I went out with a few just for what I could get. To facilitate this I passed my driving test and bought an old 100E Ford Anglia for thirty pounds. It was in fair condition and needed little doing to it. I repainted it by hand – why I do not know. I picked up the girl of the moment and drove out into the countryside, on the Goldcliff road. I found a secluded, quiet spot into which I reversed the car, and the bushes sprang closed behind me. Lacking finesse, it was "put out, or get out" so both of us started grappling in the back. It helped to pass the time while growing up.

Later I sold my car for ten pounds. It had not been right since I sank it. What a night that was! The rain was teeming down and a policeman stood in the middle of the road trying to warn drivers from driving into a flooded road, under a bridge. I drove around the policeman... and under the bridge. Stuck in the flood, my car stopped and floated sideways over the deepest part, a fountain gushing up from the handbrake as the car settled. I climbed out into waist-deep water to the applause of an appreciative crowd. The peed-off policeman, rain bouncing off every part of him, kindly said, "Don't cry, son, it will only make things worse."

It was about this time that the Smith family – Lyndon, Aunty Glad and Uncle Tom – moved from Nash Road to a larger house in Ladyhill Road, in Alway Estate. The house was on the corner of Penkin Hill. It had a small, concreted front garden, but a large back garden with a garage at the bottom. The garage was on the site of the field that was once home to the dapple-grey carthorse. The garden also had two sheds. Lyndon converted one into a smart hairdressing salon. He was a trained and experienced hairdresser and had been working in a barber shop. After the move, Lyndon lost his job as a barber; the rumour was that he was too slow and chatted too much to the clients. As he was a popular chap the local lads fixed him up with a labouring job at Spencer Works. Soon Lyndon was cutting hair in the mess room for a few shillings a time. In the evenings he dressed the hair of the local ladies in the salon in his garden. He was slow, but he was good. His appointment book was full for weeks ahead.

Lyndon had his Spencer Works salary, money from cutting hair at work, money from his salon and money from the hair products that he sold. Lyndon Smith Enterprises was by then a lucrative concern. He did not smoke, drink or own a car. Some of his income he gave to his mother, some he spent on smart clothes and whatever took his fancy; the rest he saved. Late evening, after

Lyndon had finished with the ladies, the gang drifted up to his salon for free haircuts. We had been having free haircuts for years. Lyndon worked away at our hair, telling jokes and the latest gossip he had gleaned from the ladies. Now and again the devil took him: once he finished one side of our heads, leaving the other side untouched. He then packed up his tools.

"Come back tomorrow if we wanted the other side doing," he said, and no amount of persuasion caused him to stop giggling and finish our hair. We made our way home, slinking from shadow to shadow, with Lyndon's chortles fading in the distance.

Lyndon had schemes; often they were grandiose, always they worked. One evening I was sitting at home when the doorbell rang. Mam answered.

"Hello, Lyndon," I heard.

"Hello, Aunty Marge, Uncle Bill." The latter yelled over Mam's shoulder at Dad, who was in the kitchen.

"I've got something to tell you, but you must keep it secret. Is Big Mouth in?"

"I'm in the back room," I shouted.

Lyndon came in, followed by Mam and Dad.

"This is important, you must tell no one," Lyndon kicked off. "Dad must not know."

To emphasise this he nonchalantly put his finger under my nose and raised me to my toes. Standing on tiptoe I gave Lyndon my full attention.

"Dad is retiring soon," Lyndon continued. "I am throwing him a retirement party. I have booked the church hall, and all family, friends, neighbours and his work mates will be there. You must come."

"How about the gang?" I said from under his finger.

"Well, yes, we have to have some entertainment later on," replied Lyndon. The gang were all well known to Uncle Tom and Aunty Glad, who referred to us individually and collectively as "silly young buggers". Everyone in Lliswerry and Alway were soon in on the plot, except Uncle Tom, who became irritated and frustrated by the glances, whispers and giggles. I am sure he was on his way to developing a persecution complex.

Come the night and Lyndon had decked out the church hall. All the chairs were in place facing the stage. On the stage were tables and more chairs. By early evening the hall was packed. Meanwhile, at home, two hundred metres away, Lyndon and Aunty Glad were having problems. Uncle Tom had been told there was a 'do' in the church hall, and that he must attend. Uncle Tom's thoughts were, *Bugger the do, I'm staying home with my feet up*. It took a lot of combined nagging, threatening, bribing and cajoling to get him washed, changed and out. Complaining all the way he walked to the church, closely flanked by Aunty Glad and Lyndon. As he entered the church hall everyone shut up, stood up, clapped and launched into *For he's a jolly good fellow*. Dazed and bemused, Uncle Tom was led along the aisle and onto the stage. Speeches were given, presents were presented, and people clapped, cheered and sang. Uncle Tom spent the evening dabbing his eyes. Lyndon's esteem went up a few notches in the community.

"Bit strange at times mind you, but a lovely man. Thinks a lot of his parents. Does a nice hair cut too!"

All the guys at the YMCA weight-lifting club went for

a Friday beer. The more refined guys also went for a Saturday beer. On a warm, summer night we often walked up the dirt path of Lawrence Hill, through the trees over the ridge, down past fields into Caerleon, where there were some pleasant pubs.

A Saturday beer with the less refined guys was dangerous and I only went with them once. Gate crashing dances and beating up bouncers was not my idea of fun. Nor was eating a meal and running away without paying – it gave me indigestion. Chinese restaurants and Indian curry houses were the targets. In we staggered, full to the brim with beer. Tables near the door always sported reserved signs, and it took me a while to work that one out: if we looked suspicious they did not let us sit near the door. In Chinese restaurants the service was always poor; one bored girl taking orders and serving, one little man lounging at the till, one over-worked chef in the kitchen shouting to himself, and that seemed all. But the moment the first runner legged it, there were Chinese everywhere, armed with just about everything. A dozen of them appeared. The Chinese were stayers too; they kept up a hot pursuit and running fight for miles. Rushing in, jabbering, trying to hold one person – catch one and the police would know who the others were, was their thinking. To stand and fight was dangerous; these guys were armed.

The Indians were not as much fun; their hearts were not in it. A feeble twenty-metre chase by two unarmed men and that was it. They went back inside muttering and probably spat in the cat meat curry. By cat meat, I mean cat. Cat meat in a tin costs money, but a stray cat costs nothing. The South Wales papers carried stories of Indian and Chinese restaurants being fined for serving up dogs, cats, pet food and other suspect meat. The fur was made into gloves, the bones made soup and the innards fed the fish kept in a barrel out back. Nothing was wasted, very admirable. What the heck, it tasted marvellous.

11. Starting To Grow Up

At sixteen, I had five poor O-level passes behind me, no ambition, and my parents and grandparents thought that I should do something respectable. The Youth Employment Office arranged an interview for me with Mr Myatt, the manager of the National Provincial Bank. Mr Myatt sent me to the London head office for an interview. Head office either liked the look of me or were desperate, for I was employed as a junior clerk in the Newport branch.

It was awful. From my first day of work Mam was onto me for board and lodging money: two pounds ten shillings a week, almost all my pittance. I had been better off as a schoolboy. Mr Myatt, his assistant Mr Mole and chief accountant Mr Hatcher were charming people, but a generation too late. The other staff members were friendly, but followed in their masters' footsteps.

I felt confined, caged, penned in perpetual gloom. The work, the people, the ambience and discipline were not me. It was redolent of Dickens. One job they did give me was to help with the cash run to the main post office. Notes of all denominations were sorted, counted and placed in a large, thick, canvas bag. A red and white sticker was put on this bag: HVP – highly valuable parcel. Why advertise it? Two people carried the bag, another two acted as escort. We walked it the hundred metres to the post office, going in through the back entrance. One of us had a whistle, the other a truncheon. I preferred the truncheon and hoped someone would try and rob us. It would probably have been someone I knew from the YMCA, in which case I would have worked a deal. I lasted in the job for two and a half months, and one of those was my notice.

One was judged to be lazy, work shy, a wastrel, if unemployed for more than a week. Fortunately, jobs were easy to find. Uncle Harry, Dad's cousin in Dewstow Street, worked for the Department of Employment. He arranged an interview for me with the research department of the Llanwern Steelworks, or Spencer Works. Later it was owned by Richard, Thomas and Baldwin, and after nationalisation it became British Steel. There were other steelworks in Newport then; the place was bustling. Everyone who wanted a job had a job. There was money, people were happy, and the town was clean and thriving.

The research department was at Pye Corner, near where we had gathered blackberries years before. The site stood across the road from an overgrown, Second World War barrage balloon site. It must have been a cushy posting for many a young soldier, because it was a quiet, out of the way place. In the 1940s it was really out in the country, however enemy planes did have to fly near it to attack Newport docks. My journey to work was easy: we took turns to take our cars, and on a nice summer's day we walked.

There were often work social events. These were very

well supported, for team motivation and morale were high. Men and women pitched up at a local pub on a Friday night to dance, tell jokes, eat chicken and chips and drink too much. It was boisterous but never crude; a foul word in front of a woman earned a rebuke from anyone who heard it. We were not prudes – the jokes and gossip proved that – but we had certain values. The women laughed at the jokes, told their own, drank beer, talked about the men's butts and speculated on size. My five years at Pye Corner went by quickly and happily. I enjoyed the work and I liked the people.

Me, aged 19

One of our projects was to roll steel thin enough to compete with aluminium foil. For this we built a lean-to against one of the workshops, cast a foundation and mounted a rolling mill on it. The rolling mill was very small, salvaged from a steelworks in the Midlands. We experimented with various types of steel and lubrications. Finally, using tin-plated steel with a palm oil lubrication, we succeeded in achieving the thickness we wanted. A steelworks in America had recently boasted in a journal of the thickness they had achieved. Ours was thinner than theirs. We were so excited that we typed a letter on a piece of our steel foil and sent it off to the American steelworks. The problem was, while our steel was as thin as aluminium foil, it was harder. It would not form to shape and it cut fingers.

Douglas, Me, Geoffrey, Philip in front, circa 1969

The 1960s was a decade of dramatic cultural and moral change. It was a time of free love, drugs and of youth making themselves heard. We had the miniskirt, the Beatles, the Rolling Stones and the King – the one and only Elvis Presley. I was not interested in music. I rarely listened to it and I purchased only a few records, although I did think that Elvis was good. The miniskirt was a different story; I was very interested. The newspaper photographs of pretty girls wearing miniskirts were very appealing. My parents thought the miniskirt was silly, my grandparents thought that it was disgusting. A few Newport girls plucked up the courage to wear it. They were not good advertisements for it. The few I saw in Newport should have stayed in of a night.

The 1960s had the Vietnam War too, an unjustified, unnecessary intrusion by the United States. However, at the time I was all for it; the commies had to be stopped and the good old yanks were the ones to do it. All my family, friends and colleagues felt the same way – we had been brainwashed.

In 1968 I became twenty-one years of age. I was old enough to vote. I did not vote because I had, even then, formed the opinion that all politicians are corrupt, grubby, self-serving little idiots. Over the following decades I experienced nothing that made me want to change this opinion.

At eighteen years of age, whilst working at Pye Corner, I started 'tech'; in other words I went to Newport Technical College of Further Education. Companies had an obligation to give youngsters 'day release', one day off a week for studies. My first attempt was general science. I failed. I next failed O level chemistry. I had no interest in either subject. I was just trying to keep others happy, but no one was happy and I was miserable. I was given a final chance, another year to prove myself. I chose mechanical engineering, in which I had some interest. My qualifications were not enough to get me into the two-year Ordinary National Certificate (ONC) course, but at the last moment the college relented. They needed bodies to make the numbers up, as it was not a popular course. So there I was, with others who were not all that interested. Wednesday was our day release at the college building in Clarence Place, with two hours of technical drawing on a Thursday evening in Corporation Road School.

During the first term my interest grew and I began to follow the lessons, taking notes and putting more care into my homework. I knew I had passed the first year. Then, for the first time in my life, I applied myself. That summer, before the start of the second academic year, I put time aside between work, physical training and socialising, to study. I went through my first year notes, every subject from day one to the end. I went over them time and again, until I knew all homework and examination questions, admittedly by dint of memory and by adhering to known formulae. I hit the second year running and kept up the pace.

At this time my brother Geoffrey was in the upper sixth at St Julian's, and was applying to universities to read mathematics. At the steel works I had seen university graduates doing vacation work there and also working as new recruits. They had hope, they had confidence, they were outgoing and worldly. Above all, they were treated with respect. This gave me an idea. I contacted the university clearing house, UCCA, and asked whether any university accepted an ONC entry. A lot did, so I wrote to the admissions tutors at all of them.

They sent me their entry criteria for ONC candidates. These were all in the same ballpark: a minimum of eighty percent in Maths, no mark less than sixty percent, and attendance of at least ninety-five percent. High, but achievable.

I put my heart into it. I had not taken any vacation in my first year of study, so I had three weeks carried over. I approached my boss, Alan McCrum, a first-class honours graduate. I told him my intention and asked to take six weeks' paid leave that year, together with two weeks' unpaid leave, all in one lump. He peered at me over his pipe, and agreed.

I dropped all my hobbies and interests. I dropped all my friends. I studied. In my final term I understood the work; I did not need to doggedly follow formulae or memorised methods. I knew what caused what and why what followed what. I went through those examinations with confidence.

On the walk home, after writing my last paper, I knew I had done it. I felt light, I floated, the world was a sunny, wonderful place. I arrived home. I told Mam I had passed and was off to university. I put my things away, changed and walked over to the Spencer Works Club for a beer. It was early, before licensed opening time, but that did not stop the staff serving people they knew. The club was open anyway, for snooker, television and other things. The mother of my mate, Ashley, served behind the bar. I had a pint of bitter. It was the best I had ever drunk.

I telephoned for my results and telephoned again and again until they were available, as I needed confirmation to finalise my place at university. Finally I heard: Maths, eighty-five percent and an overall average of ninety percent. The tech had confirmed one hundred percent attendance. I stood at the bottom of the stairs on a bright, sunny day and with trembling fingers I telephoned Mr Marter, admissions tutor at the mechanical engineering department of the University of Surrey.

"Well done, Mr Hughes," he said. "We will see you in September."

I enjoyed tech, but because of what tech was and because of who I was, I had no close friends there. For one day a week, I did not need any. I had acquaintances with whom I drank Horlicks in a nearby café, but that was it. I briefly had a girlfriend there – obliging lass – but she dumped me. My initial feeling was that technical college was for no-hopers; there was no pressure to attend, less to learn. It was about going through the motions and I now wanted more than that. Maybe my distance from the other students there was my effort to break out.

Both Geoffrey and I were starting university that term. My parents were very pleased, my grandfather was pleased, my grandmother was ecstatic; she told everyone. My parents were impressed by people with what they called 'letters after their name'. Within a few years their sons clocked up three honours degrees, two master's, and more letters. My parents stopped being impressed by people with letters after their name.

My work colleagues were genuinely pleased for me; Alan McCrum was thrilled. They made a collection and bought me a tracksuit, matching vest and socks and running shoes.

I had dropped out of my gang in order to study. To them I was now someone different, 'a brainy bastard'.

Except for Lyndon, I did not see any of them again.

At twenty-two I became a university undergraduate. I knew I could do things, if I applied myself. That year saw a new me: not fatty, not scaredy cat, not a thick no-hoper. I was confident, handsome, fit, strong and going places.

I applied for my student grant. As I had been, supposedly, self supporting for five years I received the full grant: four hundred and forty-four pounds a year – a large sum in those days – which covered books, accommodation and subsistence. In addition, the council paid my tuition fees and student union fees. I had the money I had saved from my work – not much, but some. I sold my air guns, bows, knives, duplicate stamp collection, comic collection and old magazines to raise more money. I resigned from British Steel. I packed my case, packed the family coffee percolator and was ready to go.

A student of the University of Surrey

My parents drove me to Guildford. They had a Jaguar 3.4 SS; it was their treat to themselves for working hard and having no vices. It was off-white with dark red trim, leather bucket seats and all the extras. On the journey to Guildford I sat in the back, excited, yet apprehensive.

As a teenager I had looked up at the few commercial aeroplanes that flew over my part of Newport and felt an urge to travel. Newport was no longer for me; I had outgrown it. I wanted adventure, travel and new experiences.

Epilogue

I cannot remember it raining in my teenage summers. I am sure that it did, but it seemed to me that the sun shone every day. Birds twittered in hedges and dragonflies buzzed around us. Those were good days; really happy, wonderful days. I was carefree, not a worry in the world – except for exams and girlfriends. We filled those days to the brim with interesting and exciting activities.

Now, sometimes of a summer evening, as I stare absent-mindedly through the window with my brain in neutral and my mouth ajar, a shadow, or sunbeam, or rustle will stir my memory. Then, for a brief moment, I can picture life as it was in my youth. I hear the faint whisper of people talking across the years. I hear insects buzzing as they once did. Eerily I smell grass, hay and flowers, as they smelt all those years ago. I almost feel the breeze that blew across our parks, fields and woods. For a few fleeting seconds I am decades in the past – it seems so real. I do not remember the bad things, the accidents, sickness and misfortunes.

Maybe it's a question of temperament, not how the world is. Youngsters these days like a day out in the city, shopping, watching films and playing on the computer. I do not suppose there is anything wrong with that. After all, growing old is mandatory but growing up is optional.

In 1973, at the age of twenty-five, I obtained an honours degree in mechanical engineering. In 1996 I became a member of the Institution of Mechanical Engineers, hence I became a chartered engineer. After my name I can write: B.Sc.(hons), CEng, MIMechE. I tried it a few times to get the feel of it and to savour it, but I soon gave up.

Geoffrey obtained an honours and a master's in mathematics. Douglas set up his own business related to computer programming. Philip achieved an honours and a master's in engineering. All told, not bad for a working-class family brought up in a small, cramped house.

I met my future wife at university. We married in 1975, had two daughters, and divorced twenty-eight years later. In between all this I worked overseas, starting in South Africa, to which we emigrated. After South Africa I drifted into contract work, leaving my family in England while I played abroad. This was one reason for the divorce. My eldest daughter emigrated to Australia. At the time of writing my youngest daughter and my two granddaughters live but a few metres away from my present home in Sutton.

The last time I went to Arley was in 1991, for Uncle Jim's funeral. The time before that was 1961, for Nana Knight's funeral. Unfortunately I was in South Africa when Grandma Hughes died on 21 November 1976. My last memories of her are of a kind, robust, roly-poly creature, with small but warm eyes. I see her even today sitting in her wooden chair in the corner by the fire, arms folded, rocking from side to side, her tea-cosy hat on her head.

I usually see my brothers, their wives and my seven nieces and nephews at Christmas in Newport when we all visit. At the time of writing, Geoffrey and Douglas live in England and Philip lives in the valleys. In my middle and old age, after my divorce, I tried my best to visit my parents every Christmas. There is something soothing about lying abed in a room one slept in as a child, with Mam and Dad still next door. On these visits Mam waited on me hand, foot and finger. I enjoyed being spoiled and took full advantage.

Sadly my father died in 2011, aged eighty-nine. My mother still lives in the house, which I now own, and I plan to retire to it. The house has changed: there is double-glazing and fitted carpets throughout and central heating. A porch has been added to the front of the house and a conservatory to the rear, which leads to a shower, toilet, store and garage. What was once a cold, cramped home for six people, is now a warm and spacious home to my mother, who sits in the porch watching the world pass by.

I saw Lyndon infrequently at one stage, but lost contact with him a few years before his death in 1997. Uncle Harry still lives four houses away from my mother and I occasionally see Patricia, who stayed in Newport and remains a friend. My other childhood friends I have not seen since 1969.

As for Newport, it was once a tatty town with steelworks and other heavy industry. It is now a tatty city with next to nothing. Still, despite its faults and despite my travels, it is home.

OTHER BOOKS BY
DAVID HUGHES

books by people living abroad for people living abroad

Lightning Source UK Ltd.
Milton Keynes UK
UKOW041953251112

202752UK00002B/1/P